Shine

Judy Garton-Sprenger • Philip Prowse
Carolyn Barraclough • Hara Yiannakopoulou

Grammar
Book
1

MAP OF THE BOOK

Introduction to the student		page 4
List of irregular verbs		page 5

UNIT 1	**PEOPLE AND PLACES**	
Lesson 1	Present simple *to be* - questions: *What? Where? How old?* personal pronouns; possessive adjectives	page 6
Lesson 2	Present simple *to be* - negative, questions, short answers question *Who?* Plurals	page 8
Lesson 3	Present simple: affirmative: *like, love, hate, live, speak*	page 10
Lesson 4	Use Your Grammar	page 12
Lesson 5	Test Yourself	page 14

UNIT 2	**THINGS**	
Lesson 1	Present simple: negative, questions, short answers, *but/or/and*	page 16
Lesson 2	Present simple: *have got*: affirmative, negative, *a/an, some, any*	page 18
Lesson 3	*Have got*: questions and short answers *Can I?*: requests and permission, *one*	page 20
Lesson 4	Use Your Grammar	page 22
Lesson 5	Test Yourself	page 24

UNIT 3	**SPORT**	
Lesson 1	Present continuous: affirmative	page 26
Lesson 2	*There is/There are/There isn't/There aren't* Prepositions of place: *in/on*	page 28
Lesson 3	Possessive *'s*; Possessive pronouns; question *Whose? Let's...*	page 30
Lesson 4	Use Your Grammar	page 32
Lesson 5	Test Yourself	page 34

UNIT 4	**ANIMALS**	
Lesson 1	Can: affirmative, negative, questions, short answers	page 36
Lesson 2	Present continuous: questions, short answers, negative	page 38
Lesson 3	Comparative adjectives: *-er, than*	page 40
Lesson 4	Use Your Grammar	page 42
Lesson 5	Test Yourself	page 44

UNIT 5	**TIME AND SPACE**	
Lesson 1	Prepositions of time; present simple: routines, *usually*	page 46
Lesson 2	Present simple: routines present continuous: *now*	page 48
Lesson 3	*Is/Are there...?* + short answers question *How many?* prepositions of place: *next to, near, opposite*	page 50
Lesson 4	Use Your Grammar	page 52
Lesson 5	Test Yourself	page 54

2

UNIT 6	**FREE TIME**	
Lesson 1	*Would like* + noun/infinitive	page 56
	this/that/these/those; countable and uncountable nouns	
Lesson 2	*-ing, like, love, hate + ing, good at + ing*	page 58
Lesson 3	Comparative adjectives: *more* + adjective	page 60
	questions *How much is it? Which one?*	
Lesson 4	Use Your Grammar	page 62
Lesson 5	Test Yourself	page 64

UNIT 7	**A LONG TIME AGO**	
Lesson 1	Past simple: *to be:* affirmative, negative,	page 66
	questions, short answers	
	Prepositions of time: *ago, there was/there were*	
	Prepositions of place: *at, in*	
Lesson 2	Past simple: regular verbs: affirmative	page 68
Lesson 3	Past simple: regular verbs: negative	page 70
	questions, short answers	
Lesson 4	Use Your Grammar	page 72
Lesson 5	Test Yourself	page 74

UNIT 8	**GHOSTS**	
Lesson 1	Past simple: irregular verbs: affirmative	page 76
Lesson 2	Past simple: regular and irregular verbs:	page 78
	negative and questions	
Lesson 3	*Why? Because, too* + adjective/adverb	page 80
Lesson 4	Use Your Grammar	page 82
Lesson 5	Test Yourself	page 84

UNIT 9	**AROUND THE WORLD**	
Lesson 1	Adverbs of frequency: *always, usually,*	page 86
	often, sometimes, never	
Lesson 2	Superlative adjectives	page 88
Lesson 3	Future: *going to:* affirmative, negative	page 90
	questions and short answers	
Lesson 4	Use Your Grammar	page 92
Lesson 5	Test Yourself	page 94

Welcome to Shine Grammar 1!

Shine Grammar 1 is a special book to help you to understand grammar.

Who is this book for?

It's for students like you who want to know more about English grammar.
Shine Grammar 1 explains the rules of grammar and gives you lots of examples, so that you can do your grammar exercises more easily.

How do I use this book?

You can use **Shine Grammar 1** together with **Shine 1** Student's Book.
Shine Grammar 1 follows the Units and lessons in the Student's Book and gives you extra grammar information for each lesson.
You can also use **Shine Grammar 1** with any other English Student's Book.
As you work with your Student's Book, you can use **Shine Grammar 1** to learn more about the grammar points in each lesson.

What is in the book?

Shine Grammar 1 is full of explanations that are easy to understand. There are lots of examples and plenty of exercises so that you can practise as you learn.
In every fourth lesson there are exercises so that you can use all the important grammar you have learnt.
Then you can test yourself to see how good your grammar is!

What's special about Shine Grammar 1?

- You don't have to learn lots of new words for **Shine Grammar 1**. The book uses words you already know.

- The rules and explanations are easy to understand and learn.

- **Shine Grammar 1** tells you everything you need to know about English grammar at your level.

- With **Shine Grammar 1**, grammar is **EASY** and **FUN!**

Enjoy the book!

Irregular Verbs

Infinitive	Past simple	Infinitive	Past simple
be	was, were	let	let
beat	beat	make	made
bend	bent	mean	meant
buy	bought	meet	met
catch	caught	put	put
choose	chose	read	read
come	came	ride	rode
cost	cost	ring	rang
do	did	run	ran
draw	drew	say	said
drink	drank	see	saw
drive	drove	shine	shone
eat	ate	sing	sang
fall	fell	sit	sat
feel	felt	sleep	slept
fight	fought	speak	spoke
find	found	spell	spelt/spelled
fly	flew	spend	spent
get	got	stand	stood
give	gave	swim	swam
go	went	take	took
have	had	tell	told
hear	heard	think	thought
hold	held	understand	understood
know	knew	wear	wore
lead	led	win	won
learn	learned/learnt	write	wrote
leave	left		

LESSON 1 *Welcome to London*

1 Present simple: *to be*

We can use the verb **to be** before adjectives. We can say, for example, how you feel about starting school again after the summer holidays.

> **Are you** happy?
> Yes, **I'm** happy. **I'm not** sad.

Affirmative	Contractions
I am	I'm
you are	you're
he is	he's
she is	she's
it is	it's
we are	we're
you are	you're
they are	they're

Top Tip!

We call this verb **to be**. That's the name of the verb – but we don't use the word **be** at all in the present simple. The word **be** is the **infinitive** form of the verb. You learn about infinitives later. The important thing to remember now is that you never use the word **be** with personal pronouns. The verb **to be** uses **am, is** or **are** in the present simple.

2 Personal pronouns

I
you
he
she
it
we
you
they

These words tell us which person or people we are talking about. They tell us **who** is doing something or **who** somebody is.
Personal pronouns always go before the verb.

> **She** is Susan.
> **They** are reading.

3 Possessive adjectives

my
your
his
her
its
our
your
their

These words tell us who something belongs to. They answer the question **whose?**

> This is **my mother**.
> **His book** is on the desk.

4 *What? Where? How old?*

We use these words to get more information about something or somebody.
We use **What?** to find out more about things, actions and situations.
We use **Where?** to find out more about places.
We use **How old?** to find out about age.

> **What** is this?   It's a great grammar book!
> **Where** is the book?   It's in my bag.
> **How old** are you?   I'm fourteen.

1 Complete the dialogue.

Jim: Hello. (0) *I'm* Jim. What's your name?

Marianna: I'm Marianna. Where (1) _____ you from?

Jim: (2) _____ from New York. Where (3) _____ you from?

Marianna: I (4) _____ from London.

Jim: How old (5) _____ you?

Marianna: (6) _____ thirteen. How old (7) _____ you?

Jim: (8) _____ fifteen.

2 Look and write questions about Alice. Use these words to help you.

| colour favourite How old What |

Alice

Sydney
Australia
blue
14
Australian

Alice

0   *Where is Alice from?*   She's from Sydney, Australia.

1   _____   It's blue.

2   _____   She's fourteen.

3   _____   Yes, she is.

Now write answers about Antonio.

Antonio

Venice
Italy
red
13
Italian

Antonio

00   How old is Antonio?   *He's thirteen.*

4   What's his favourite colour?   _____

5   Where is he from ?   _____

6   Is he Italian?   _____

3 Put apostrophes in the correct places.

0   Mariannas from London. *Marianna's from London.*

1   Shes thirteen.   _____

2   Whats her favourite sport?_____

3   How olds Jim?   _____

4   Hes American.   _____

5   His favourite colours green._____

6   Wheres he from?   _____

4 Write sentences with these words.

| his her my our their your |

0   bag/Maria   *This is her bag.*

1   radio/Daniel   _____

2   book/Roberto and Carla_____

3   town/us   _____

4   favourite programme/Anna_____

5   watch/you   _____

6   favourite sport/me   _____

LESSON 2 — *Who's that?*

❶ Present simple *to be*: make negative questions, short answers and negative answers

This is how we make negative sentences, ask questions or give short answers, using the verb **to be**.

Negative	Contractions	Questions	Short answers
I am not	I'm not	Am I?	Yes, I am./No, I'm not.
you are not	you aren't	Are you?	Yes, you are./No, you aren't.
he is not	he isn't	Is he?	Yes, he is./No, he isn't.
she is not	she isn't	Is she?	Yes, she is./No, she isn't.
it is not	it isn't	Is it?	Yes, it is./No, it isn't.
we are not	we aren't	Are we?	Yes, we are./No, we aren't.
you are not	you aren't	Are you?	Yes, you are./No, you aren't.
they are not	they aren't	Are they?	Yes, they are./ No, they aren't.

> **Top Tip!**
> Remember to change the order of the words when you ask a question. The verb goes before the personal pronoun in the question.
>   **You are** Daniel. – **Are you** Daniel? (Yes, I am./No, I'm not.)
>   **She is** happy. – **Is she** happy? (Yes, she is./No, she isn't.)

❷ *Who*

We use the word **who** when we want information about a person or people. We only use **who** to ask about *people* – not to ask about things or animals.
    Who is he? He's my brother.
    Who is she? She's Mary.

> **Top Tip!**
> When we want to know the identity of a man or a woman we can use **Who's that?** and we can answer using *it*.
>   **Who's that?** It's Tom.
>   **Who's that?** It's Anne.

❸ Plural

For most nouns in English we make the plural by adding **– s** to the end of the word.
    book – book**s**
    house – house**s**
But for some words we make the plural in other ways. For words that end in a **consonant + y** – take away the **– y** and add – **ies** to the end of the word.
    party – part**ies**
    study – stud**ies**

But remember – for words that end in a **vowel + y** – just add **– s** to the end of the word.
    boy – boy**s**
There are also some irregular plurals.
    man – **men**
    woman – **women**
    person – **people**
    child – **children**

❶ Complete the sentences.

0	Who are you?	*I'm Carla.*	
1	_____ he?	_____	Martin.
2	_____ she?	_____	Silvia.
3	_____ they?	_____	Carla and Roberto.
4	_____ you?	_____	Anna and Maria.
5	_____ they?	_____	Tom and Daniel.

2 Make these sentences negative.

0 Alice is from Australia.   *Alice isn't from Australia.*

1 It's Monday today. _____

2 I'm Spanish. _____

3 There are twenty competitors. _____

4 Our favourite sports are basketball and football. _____

5 This is my dog. _____

6 Rio and London are Spanish cities. _____

7 Fifty people are at the party. _____

3 Write short answers.

0 Are you ten years old?

   No, I'm not.

1 Are you English?

_____

2 Is it two o'clock?

_____

3 Are your shoes black?

_____

4 Is your teacher a man?

_____

5 Are you a girl?

_____

6 Are you a boy?

_____

4 These children are competitors in a race.

Write what numbers they are.

Chris 93   Sarah 37   Emma 68   Robert 72

     0   **1**   **2**   **3**

0 *Chris is number ninety three.*

1 _____

2 _____

3 _____

4 _____

5 _____

6 _____

Tom 40   Cara 55   Tony 89

     4   **5**   **6**

LESSON 3 — *I like this music*

---

1 Present simple: affirmative

We form the affirmative of the present simple tense of regular verbs like this:

Affirmative

I like
you like
he like**s**
she like**s**
it like**s**
we like
you like
they like

Top Tip!

Remember that for the **present simple affirmative** add the – **s** to the end of the verb for the third person singular forms (**he, she, it**).

We use the **present simple** tense to talk about things that do not change – and to talk about our likes and dislikes.

> I am English.
> She likes tennis.

2 *live, speak*

We use these verbs when we are talking about things that do not change.

> I **live** in London.
> She **speaks** Spanish.

3 *like, love, hate*

We use these verbs to talk about likes or dislikes.

> I **like** basketball.
> They **love** Johnny Depp.
> He **hates** school.

---

1 Look and complete the sentences.

Name	love	like	hate	Name	love	like	hate
Bill				Marina			
Sarah				Tony			
Claudia				Sissy			

love   **like**

0   Bill *loves basketball.*

1   Tony _____   5   Tony _____

2   Claudia _____   6   Sissy _____

3   Marina and Sissy _____   7   Marina and Bill _____

4   Sarah _____   8   Sarah and Claudia _____

2   Look again and write sentences with *hate.*

0   *Bill and Marina hate* running.

1   _____ football.

2   _____ tennis.

3   _____ volleyball.

4   _____ swimming.

3   Complete the sentences with the correct form of the verb in brackets.

0   I *like Claudia.* She's my friend. (like)

1   They _____ Italy – it's a wonderful country. (love)

2   He _____ in a city in Spain. (live)

3   She _____ Ricky Martin. (love)

4   They _____ tennis. (hate)

5   You _____ English. (speak)

6   Jim and George _____ music. (love)

7   Marianna _____ Spanish, English and Italian. (speak)

4   Make these sentences plural.

0   My teacher is wonderful.   *My teachers are wonderful.*

1   The child loves swimming.   _____

2   The man hates football.   _____

3   The woman speaks three languages.   _____

4   My friend likes rock music.   _____

5   The Turkish competitor is at the games. _____

1 PEOPLE AND PLACES

LESSON 4 *Use Your Grammar*

Lesson 4 of every Unit in **Shine Grammar 1** helps you learn how to use your grammar when you do writing exercises.

Now you are going to write about yourself.

Complete these sentences about someone you know using the grammar in **Unit** 1.

Personal details

My name is _____ .
I am from _____ .
I live in _____ .
My birthday is on _____ .
I am _____ years old.

Abilities and things I always do

I speak English.
I play football.
I walk to school.

Preferences

I like _____ .
I love _____ .
I hate _____ .
My favourite _____ is/are _____ .
(My favourite food is cheese.
My favourite sports are football
and tennis.)

Now you have all the information you need to write a description of that person.

1 **Read the letter from Marianna to her new penfriend.**

Dear Francesca,

Hi! I'm Marianna. I'm thirteen and I live with my mum, dad and sister in London, England.
I like sport. My favourite sport is basketball – I love it!
My sister, Helena, is nineteen. She loves parties and she hates sport!
This is my mum. She likes books.
This is my dad. He's from the north of England. He loves music and he likes football.
What do you like?
Please write to me.

Love,
Marianna

2 Now answer the questions about Marianna and her family.

1 Who is her new penfriend? _____

2 Where is her dad from? _____

3 What's her favourite sport? _____

4 Who is Helena? _____

5 How old is she? _____

6 Where is Marianna from? _____

7 Is she fifteen years old? _____

3 Complete the letter using the words in the box.

your	hates	is	love	likes	What	live	my	is	are	play

Dear Helen,

Hi! My name (1) _____ Peter. I'm fifteen years old and I (2) _____ in Paris with my mum, my dad and (3) _____ sister, Christine.

I (4) _____ sport. My favourite sport (5) _____ football. I (6) _____ football every Saturday. My sister (7) _____ football! She (8) _____ tennis. (9) _____ sports do you like?

How old (10) _____ you? When is (11) _____ birthday?

Please write a letter to me.

Bye,

Peter.

4 Now write a letter to Peter about you and your family.

Dear Peter,

_____

_____

_____

_____

_____

_____

_____

_____

LESSON 5 *Test Yourself*

1 **Write questions from the words below.
Then write the answers.**

Question	**Answer**

0 you are How old
How old are you?   *I'm eleven.*

1 the date today What's

_____?   _____

2 When's birthday your

_____?   _____

3 are Where from you

_____?   _____

4 sport What's favourite your

_____?   _____

5 teacher Who your is

_____?   _____

2 **Underline the correct answer.**

0 Astrid **is/are** an alien.
1 Arnie and Astrid **is/are** aliens.
2 Tony **like/likes** football.
3 Marina and Sissy **love/loves** volleyball.
4 Maria **live/lives** in São Paulo.
5 Helena **hate/hates** sport.
6 Maria **love/loves** basketball.
7 Marina and Bill **like/likes** tennis.
8 Sissy and Claudia **hate/hates** football.
9 What **is/are** your favourite sport?
10 Where **is/are** you from?

14

3 **Underline the mistake in each sentence. Then correct it.**

0   That is a book. No, it <u>aren't</u>.   *That is a book. No, it <u>isn't.</u>*

1   Astrid is an alien. Yes, she's.   _____

2   My favourite sport are volleyball.   _____

3   We likes gymnastics.   _____

4   Maria likes volleyball. It's his favourite sport.   _____

5   Tom live in the USA.   _____

6   Where is you from?   _____

7   How old is they?   _____

8   We like blue. It's their favourite colour.   _____

9   Are you from England? Yes, I'm.   _____

4 **Underline the correct answer.**

0   Is she Italian?

    a. Yes, is.   **b.** Yes, she's.   <u>**c.** Yes, she is.</u>

1   Are you from New York?
    a. No, I'm not.   **b.** No, I not.   **c.** No, I are not.

2   How old is Jim?
    a. He nine.   **b.** He's nine.   **c.** He are nine.

3   Who's that?
    a. It Jim.   **b.** He is Jim.   **c.** It's Jim.

4   Are they your friends?
    a. Yes, they are.   **b.** Yes, they're.   **c.** Yes, their.

5   Where are you from?
    a. I Spanish.   **b.** I'm from Spain.   **c.** I from Spain.

6   Is he your teacher?
    a. No, he's isn't.   **b.** No, he isn't.   **c.** No, he not.

Do you like it?

1 Present simple: negative, questions and short answers

This is how we make negative sentences, questions and answers in the **present simple**.

Negative	Contractions	Questions	Short answers
I do not like	I don't like	Do I like?	Yes, I do./No, I don't.
you do not like	you don't like	Do you like?	Yes, you do./No, you don't.
he does not like	he doesn't like	Does he like?	Yes, he does./No, he doesn't.
she does not like	she doesn't like	Does she like?	Yes, she does./No, she doesn't.
it does not like	it doesn't like	Does it like?	Yes, it does./No, it doesn't.
we do not like	we don't like	Do we like?	Yes, we do./No, we don't.
you do not like	you don't like	Do you like?	Yes, you do./No, you don't.
they do not like	they don't like	Do they like?	Yes, they do./No, they don't.

Top Tip!

In the negative and in questions, the main verb does not change at all.
Remember that **do** changes to **does** for the third person singular (he, she, it).
Note that the word order changes in questions – **do/does** goes before the personal pronoun and the main verb.

He doesn't like sports.   **Does he like** sports? (Yes, he **does**./No, he **doesn't**.)

2 but/or/and

We use **but** to join two sentences with opposite or contrasting meanings.
I like swimming **but** I hate football.
She likes tennis **but** she doesn't like basketball.
We use **and** to connect two or more similar ideas together.
I love chocolate **and** cakes.
He likes London, Paris **and** Rome.
We use **or** when we are talking about a choice between two or more things.
Do you like the pink T-shirt **or** the blue T-shirt?
Do you play football **or** tennis?

1 Complete the charts with *do/does* and *don't/doesn't*.

0	I	*do*	00	I	*don't*
1	you	_____	7	you	_____
2	he	_____	8	he	_____
3	she	_____	9	she	_____
4	it	_____	10	it	_____
5	we	_____	11	we	_____
6	they	_____	12	they	_____

2 Write questions and then answer about yourself.

0   you/like/school?   *Do you like school?*   *Yes, I do.*

1   you/like/pink?

_____

2   you/like/English magazines?

_____

3   you/like/presents?

_____

4   you/like/tracksuits?

_____

5   you/like/music?   _____

6   you/like/orange?   _____

7   you/like/books?   _____

8   you/like/T-shirts?   _____

9   you/like/black?   _____

3   Write questions about sport and ask a friend.

0	running	*Do you like running?*	
1	tennis	_____?	
2	basketball	_____?	
3	football	_____?	
4	swimming	_____?	

4   Write about your friend.

0   *Jim loves running.*

1   _____

2   _____

3   _____

4   _____

CHART	love	like	don't like	hate
Bill		Madonna		Eminem
Claudia		Britney Spears		
Claudia & Bill	Ricky Martin			Tom Jones

5   Read and complete the chart.

Bill is talking...

'We like music. We love Ricky Martin, he's great, but we don't like Robbie Williams. We like Westlife's new CD very much. We hate Tom Jones.

Claudia likes Britney Spears and she loves music videos. I don't like Britney Spears very much but I quite like Madonna. Cristina Aguilera is my favourite. I love her but Claudia hates her music. I hate Eminem.

6   Look at the chart in exercise 5 and write sentences.

0   Bill *likes Madonna.*

1   He _____

2   Claudia _____

3   She _____

4   Claudia and Bill _____

5   They _____

6   They _____

2 THINGS

You've got a new sweatshirt!

1 Present simple: *have got*: affirmative and negative

We use the verb **have got** to talk about possessions.

Affirmative	Contractions	Negative	Contractions
I have got	I've got	I have not got	I haven't got
you have got	you've got	you have not got	you haven't got
he has got	he's got	he has not got	he hasn't got
she has got	she's got	she has not got	she hasn't got
it has got	it's got	it has not got	it hasn't got
we have got	we've got	we have not got	we haven't got
you have got	you've got	you have not got	you haven't got
they have got	they've got	they have not got	they haven't got

Top Tip!

The most important thing to remember is that **have** changes to **has** for the third person singular (**he**, **she**, **it**).

> I **have** got a black T-shirt.
> He **has** got a new bike.
> She **has** got a blue hat.

2 *a/an, some, any*

We use the article **a/an** to talk about one person or thing.

Reember, there are three important points.

- use **a** before nouns that begin with a consonant sound (a cat).
- use **an** before nouns that begin with a vowel sound (an ice cream, an elephant).
- never use **a/an** before plural nouns. We can only use **a/an** to talk about one thing.

With plural nouns we use **some** and **any**.

We use **some** in affirmative sentences.

> I've got **some** books.
> She's got **some** magazines.

We use **any** in negative sentences and questions.

> I haven't got **any** apples.
> Has she got **any** CDs?

1 Complete the sentences with *a* or *an*.

0   This is *a* nice room.

1   It's _____ orange tracksuit.

2   He's got _____ white sweatshirt.

3   He's _____ silly man!

4   I've got _____ Italian jacket.

5   This is _____ American computer game.

6   This is _____ great magazine.

7   She's got _____ Australian cap.

2 Complete the sentences with *a, some* or *any*.

0   Sue hasn't got *any* bars of chocolate.

1   Tom has got _____ videos.

2   Anna and Daniel have got _____ magazines.

3   Roberto hasn't got _____ postcards or stamps.

4   Martin has got _____ mountain bike.

5   Tom has got _____ new black trainers.

6   Maria has got _____ chocolate but she wants a drink.

3 Look in Silvia's bag and see what she has and hasn't got. Then write sentences.

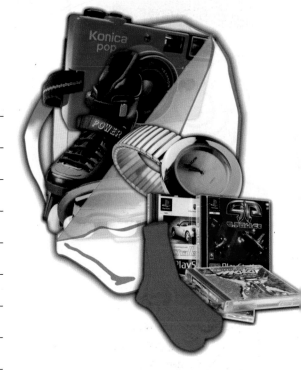

0	computer games	[✔]	*She's got some computer games.*
00	magazines	[✗]	*She hasn't got any magazines.*
1	watch	[ ]	_____
2	camera	[ ]	_____
3	cassettes	[ ]	_____
4	Walkman	[ ]	_____
5	video(s)	[ ]	_____
6	tracksuit	[ ]	_____
7	rollerblades	[ ]	_____
8	jacket	[ ]	_____
9	socks	[ ]	_____
10	cap	[ ]	_____

4 Underline the correct answer.

0 Maria _____ got a tracksuit, but it's at the hotel.
a. have   b. 've   <u>c. has</u>

1 It's his birthday, but he _____ got any presents.
a. hasn't   b. haven't   c. 've

2 I _____ got a postcard for my friend in Spain.
a. 've   b. has   c. 's

3 But I _____ got any stamps.
a. 've   b. haven't   c. hasn't

4 You _____ got any socks on.
a. haven't   b. hasn't   c. 've

5 Silvia and Daniel _____ got any money.
a. has   b. haven't   c. hasn't

6 Sue wants to listen to music,
but she _____ got her Walkman.
a. has   b. 's   c. hasn't

LESSON 3 — *Can I help you?*

1 *Have got:* questions and short answers

Questions	Short answers
Have I got?	Yes, I have./No, I haven't.
Have you got?	Yes, you have./No, you haven't.
Has he got?	Yes, he has./No, he hasn't.
Has she got?	Yes, she has./No, she hasn't.
Has it got?	Yes, it has./No, it hasn't.
Have we got?	Yes, we have./No, we haven't.
Have you got?	Yes, you have./No, you haven't.
Have they got?	Yes, they have./No, they haven't.

Don't forget – **have** changes to **has** in questions in the same way as it does in affirmative sentences.

Remember – we don't use **got** in short answers.

2 *Can I ...?* (requests and permission)

We use **can** to ask for things politely.
> **Can** I have a glass of water?
> **Can** we have a bar of chocolate?

And we also use **can** when we ask for permission to do something.
> **Can** I go out tonight?
> **Can** we play football tomorrow?

The answers are –
Yes, you can or **Yes, of course.**
No, you can't.

3 *One*

We use **one** so that we don't have to repeat the same word. We can replace the noun we are talking about with the word **one**.
> I've got a **guitar**.
> My sister has got **one** too.
> (instead of: My sister has got a guitar too.)
> Have you got a black **T-shirt** or a blue **T-shirt**?
> I've got a black **one**. (instead of: I've got a black T-shirt.)

1 Answer the questions.

0   Have you got any CDs?   *Yes, I have.*

1   Have you got a badge on your clothes today?   _____

2   Has your friend got a blue T-shirt?   _____

3   Have you got a magazine in your bag?   _____

4   Has your teacher got a jacket?   _____

5   Have your friends got any videos?   _____

6   Have you got any cassettes?   _____

7   Have your friends got sandwiches in their bags?   _____

2 **Astrid and Arnie are in Florida. What have they got in their bags? Look and answer the questions.**

Astrid   Arnie

0	Has Astrid got a cap? *No, she hasn't.*	Has Arnie got a cap? *Yes, he has.*
1	Has Astrid got a skirt? _____	Has Arnie got a shirt? _____
2	Has Astrid got a tracksuit? _____	Has Arnie got a tracksuit? _____
3	Has Astrid got any shoes? _____	Has Arnie got any trainers? _____
4	Has Astrid got a dress? _____	Has Arnie got a jacket? _____
5	Has Astrid got any socks? _____	Has Arnie got any socks? _____

3 **Look at exercise 2 again. Write questions and answers.**

0	socks	*Have they got socks?*	*Yes, they have.*
00	t-shirts	*Have they got T-shirts?*	*Arnie has got a T-shirt but Astrid hasn't got one.*
1	caps	_____	_____
2	shoes	_____	_____
3	tops	_____	_____
4	jackets	_____	_____

4 **Write questions to complete the dialogues.**

0 You want to borrow a pen. (blue)
Have you got a pen?
Yes, I've got a blue one and a red one.
Can I have the blue one, please?

1 You want to buy a T-shirt. (small)
Have _____ ?
Yes, I've got a medium one and a small one.
Can _____ ?

2 You want to borrow a pencil. (black)
Have _____ ?
Yes, I've got a grey one and a black one.
Can _____ ?

3 You want to borrow a book. (English)
Have _____ ?
Yes, I've got an English one and a French one.
Can _____ ?

4 You want to buy a tracksuit. (red)
Have _____ ?
Yes, I've got an orange one and a red one.
Can _____ ?

5 You want to borrow a ruler. (large)
Have _____ ?
Yes, I've got a small one and a large one.
Can _____ ?

Use Your Grammar

1 Present simple

When you are writing or talking to someone for the first time (to a new friend for example) you often describe yourself, your likes and dislikes and the things you always do. Now you know the best way to do this – use the **present simple**!

2 *Have got*

When you write or talk about your possessions, your family or your clothes, you can use the verb **have got**.

3 Questions

When you want to find out about somebody, you can use these question words: **when**, **where**, **who**, **what**, **how old**, or you can use the **question** form of the verbs **have got** and other verbs in the **present simple**.

And when you want to ask for something, or you want to ask to do something, don't forget to use the verb **can**.

1 **Astrid is talking about her favourite sports star. Read the text.**

I love volleyball and Arnie the Alien is my favourite volleyball player.
He is from Stella Nova, but he visits us here on Earth.
Arnie's mum and dad don't live in Stella Nova now, they live in Hula-Hula.

Arnie likes dancing and he loves volleyball, of course. He is a star competitor – he wins a lot. He doesn't like football and he hates golf.

Arnie hasn't got a tracksuit and he hasn't got any footballs, but he has got 52 volleyballs! His favourite volleyball is a purple one.

2 **Now answer the questions.**

1   Does Arnie play golf? _____

2   Has he got a mum and dad? _____

3   Do they live in Stella Nova? _____

4   Does Arnie like football? _____

5   Does he like dancing? _____

6   Does he win a lot? _____

7   Has he got a tracksuit? _____

8   Has he got any volleyballs? _____

3 **Answer these questions about yourself.**

1 Do you like Robbie Williams? _____ .

2 Do you hate computer games? _____ .

3 Do you play volleyball? _____ .

4 Have you got any black trainers? _____ .

5 Do you like swimming? _____ .

4 **Complete the sentences using the correct form of the verb in brackets.**

1 I like tennis but I _____ running. (like)

2 They've got some magazines but they _____ any videos. (have got)

3 _____ she _____ golf every day? (play)

4 Joey hates football but he _____ dancing. (love)

5 _____ you _____ a tracksuit? (have got)

5 **Write three affirmative and three negative sentences about yourself. Use the verbs *like* and *have got*.**

1 _____

2 _____

3 _____

4 _____

5 _____

6 _____

6 **Write about your favourite film star.**

_____

_____

_____

_____

_____

_____

_____

1 Underline the full forms. Then write short forms.

0   Marina <u>does not</u> like Britney Spears.   *doesn't*

1   Jim loves films. He has got lots of videos.   _____

2   I do not want a sandwich.   _____

3   They have got wonderful clothes in this shop.   _____

4   My mum has got lots of cassettes of Barry Manilow.   _____

5   We do not want to go to Washington. We want to go

    to Los Angeles.   _____

6   I have got two Italian friends – Antonio and Isabella.   _____

7   We have not got a hotel in our town.   _____

2 Complete the sentences with the correct form of *do* or *have*.

0   We *have* got a new car.

1   Look at that poor dog.

    It _____ got any food.

2   Do you like swimming?

    Yes, I _____ .

3   Have you got any money?

    Yes, I _____ .

4   They _____ got any trainers.

5   _____ Helen like tennis?

6   _____ they like the hotel?

    No, they _____ like it very much.

7   _____ she got any rollerblades? No, she _____ .

8   _____ he like your present? No, he _____ !

9   _____ we got any tennis rackets? Yes, we _____ .

3 Answer the questions with short answers.

0   Do your friends speak English?   *Yes, they do.*

1   Does your teacher like rock music?   _____

2   Have your friends got guitars?   _____

3   Have you got a cousin in Paris?   _____

4   Do you like England?   _____

5   Has your teacher got a camera?   _____

4 Underline the mistake in each sentence. Then correct it.

0   You haven't got <u>some</u> friends in London.   *You haven't got any friends in London.*

1   Helen wants some new tracksuit.   _____

2   Have you got a money?   _____

3   Please can I have any apples?   _____

4   Jim hasn't got some keys.   _____

5   Carla has got any birthday presents.   _____

5 Tick the correct sentences.

0   Sissy speaks very good Spanish.   ☑

1   Do you wants the pink T-shirt?   ☐

2   Can I have the purple, please?   ☐

3   Claudia doesn't want some new shoes.   ☐

4   Please can I have the small one?   ☐

5   Antonio wants some Italian jeans.   ☐

6   Her favourite pop star is Michael Jackson

   – she love him.   ☐

7   Do you like Brazilian food? Yes, I like. ☐

3 SPORT

LESSON 1 *She's touching her toes*

Present continuous: affirmative

We form the **present continuous** tense with the verb **be** (am/is/are) and the main verb ending **–ing**.

Affirmative	Contractions
I am watching	I'm watching
you are watching	you're watching
he is watching	he's watching
she is watching	she's watching
it is watching	it's watching
we are watching	we're watching
you are watching	you're watching
they are watching	they're watching

There are some spelling rules to remember for the ending **–ing**.

- when the main verb ends with a vowel then a consonant, for example **run** and **stop**, we double the last consonant:
  run – ru**nn**ing
  stop – sto**pp**ing

- when the main verb ends in – **e**, for example **come** and **write**, we take away the – **e** before adding **ing** –
  come – com**ing**
  write – writ**ing**

We use the **present continuous** when we talk about what is (or isn't) happening at the time when we are speaking. We can use it to talk about what people are wearing, what people are doing.
   I **am learning** English grammar now.
   We **are reading** this book at the moment.
   Look! She **is wearing** a purple jacket.

And there is one more thing to remember!
There are some verbs that we do not change into the **present continuous** tense. These verbs include **love**, **like**, **want**, **understand**, **hate**, **know**.
   I **want** some chocolate now.

---

1 Tick the correct sentences.

0 I'm playing tennis. ✓
1 You're haveing a wonderful birthday. ☐
2 He's swiming in a race. ☐
3 She's touching her toes. ☐
4 We're writting a book. ☐
5 They're sitting in the car. ☐
6 You're doeing some exercises. ☐
7 Look at the dog. It's watching television. ☐
8 I'm wearring new blue jeans. ☐
9 I'm holding my books. ☐

2 Complete the sentences.

0 *I'm* running round the track.
1 _____'s touching her toes.
2 _____ 're wearing their black tracksuits.
3 _____'re doing our exercises.
4 _____'re holding your cap.
5 _____'s touching his ear.

3 **Complete the sentences with the correct form of these verbs.**

| answer ask drink hold hold listen sit stand ~~talk~~ wear |

Martin is (0) *talking* to Carla and Roberto.

Martin is (1) _____ a question and Carla

is (2) _____ . Roberto is (3) _____ to them.

He is (4) _____ a tracksuit and (5) _____ a ball.

Martin is (6) _____ lemonade.

Martin and Roberto are (7) _____ down, but Carla is

(8) _____ up. She is (9) _____ a purple bag.

What's your name?

My name is Carla.

4 **Complete the sentences with the short form of the verb in brackets.**

0   They*'re wearing* tracksuits and trainers. (wear)

1   I _____ a letter to my penfriend. (write)

2   We _____ a new book at school. (read)

3   She _____ round the track –

     I think she _____ ! (run, win)

4   You _____ a very nice cap, I like it. (wear)

5   He _____ the window – it's very cold in here. (close)

5 **Write about what your friends and your teacher are doing now. Use some of these verbs to help you.**

| answer ask help listen read sit speak spell stand talk think wear write |

0   *My teacher is standing and she is talking to us.*

1   _____

2   _____

3   _____

4   _____

5   _____

6   _____

7   _____

8   _____

LESSON 2 *She's on the left, in lane 3*

❶ *There is / There are*

We use **there is** or **there are** to say that something exists.
We use **there is** when we are talking about one thing, and **there are** when we are talking about more than one thing.

> **There is** a book in your bag.
> **There are** some books in your bag.

For **questions** we change the word order:

> **Is there** a dog in the garden?
> **Are there** any apples on the table?

For **answers** we use:

> Yes, **there is**. / No, **there isn't**. (singular)
> and
> Yes, **there are**. / No, **there aren't**. (plural)

❷ Prepositions of place: *on, in*

We use **on** and **in** to describe where something/somebody is.
We use **on** when a thing/person is on top of something else.

> The dog is sitting **on** the chair.
> The book is **on** the desk.

We also use **on** with the words left and right.

> The road to the cinema is **on the left**.
> The books about grammar are **on the right** of the shelf.

We use **in** when a thing/person is inside a place or thing.

> The orange is **in** the bag.
> My sister is **in** the living room.

We can also use **in** with the names of towns, cities and countries.

> I live **in** London.
> My father works **in a shop**.

And we can use the phrase **in the middle**.

> My school is **in the middle** of the city.
> The table is **in the middle** of the room.

---

❶ Sue has got a lot of things in her bag. Write sentences with *There is* or *There isn't*.

0 apple   *There is an apple in her bag.*

1 elephant   _____

2 key   _____

3 notebook   _____

4 banana   _____

5 bar of chocolate   _____

6 sandwich   _____

7 watch   _____

2 **There are five more things in Sue's bag.**
Find them and write sentences.

1 *There is* _____

2 _____

3 _____

4 _____

5 _____

3 **Complete the sentences with *on* or *in*.**

0 There are eight girls *in* the swimming pool.

1 There are two tennis rackets _____ the floor.

2 My chair is _____ the right.

3 Tom is wearing a cap _____ his head.

4 Rosa is running _____ the middle lane.

5 A boy is sitting _____ the table.

6 There's a computer _____ the classroom.

4 **Make these sentences plural.**

Singular	Plural
0 There is a book on the desk.	*There are some books on the desk.*
1 There is a mountain bike in the shop.	_____
2 There is a girl in the room.	_____
3 There is a good programme on TV.	_____
00 There isn't an apple on the tree.	*There aren't any apples on the tree.*
4 There isn't a pen in her bag.	_____
5 There isn't a computer in the school.	_____
6 There isn't a telephone in her car.	_____

5 **Make these sentences negative.**

Affirmative	Negative
0 There are some boys in the shop.	*There aren't any boys in the shop.*
1 There is a television in the classroom.	_____
2 There is a clock on the wall.	_____
3 There are some runners on the track.	_____

6 **Write sentences about your classroom or bedroom.**

1 There is _____

2 There isn't _____

3 There are _____

4 There aren't _____

5 _____

6 _____

LESSON 3 *Whose seat is this?*

---

1 Possessive – 's

We use – **'s** to talk about possessions and relationships.
We add – **'s** to the end of the person's name.
> This is Jim. This is his T-shirt – This is Jim**'s** T-shirt.
> That is my mum. That is her car. – That is my mum**'s** car.
> There is Frank. That is his sister. That is Frank**'s** sister.

2 Possessive pronouns

We also use possessive pronouns to describe possessions and relationships.

mine
yours
his
hers
its
ours
yours
theirs

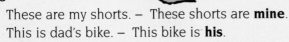

> These are my shorts. – These shorts are **mine**.
> This is dad's bike. – This bike is **his**.

3 Whose ...?

We use **whose** when we want to find out who something belongs to.
We begin the question with the word **whose**. We can use – **'s** in the answer.
> **Whose** is this racket? It's Tom**'s**.
> **Whose** are these tennis balls? They're Jenny**'s**.

We can say:
> **Whose** books are these?
> or
> **Whose** are these books?

4 Let's

When you want to suggest an activity – for example, you want to go swimming and you want your friend to go too – you can use **let's**.
> **Let's** go swimming.
> **Let's** watch television.
> **Let's** play a computer game.
> **Let's** learn some grammar.

---

1 Match.

0   This is my mum's and dad's car.
1   There is Nick's new bike.
2   I like your dress.
3   I've got a Boyzone CD.
4   We've got a computer.
5   Anna's tracksuit is in her bag.

d	a.	It's ours.
☐	b.	It's yours.
☐	c.	It's hers.
☐	d.	It's theirs.
☐	e.	It's his.
☐	f.	It's mine.

2 Complete the sentences.

0   I've got a book. It's *my* book. It's *mine*.

1   Sue's got a red bag. It's _____ bag.
    It's _____ .

2   My mother and father have got a new car. It's _____ car. It's _____ .

3   You have got three white cats.
    They're _____ cats. They're _____ .

4   My sister and I have got a big bedroom.
    It's _____ bedroom. It's _____ .

5   Jim has got some computer games.
    They're _____ computer games.
    They're _____ .

3 Look and write sentences.

0 Helen *It's Helen's Walkman.*

00 Jim *They're Jim's sunglasses.*

1 George _____

2 Paul _____

3 Sissy _____

4 Antonio _____

5 Maria _____

6 John _____

4 Write questions and answers.

0 Walkman/Helen *Whose Walkman is this?*
Is it yours, Helen? Yes, it's mine.

00 sunglasses/Marina/Jim *Whose sunglasses are these?*
Are they yours, Marina? No, they're Jim's.

1 ticket/George _____

2 basketballs/Martin/Paul _____

3 bike/Sissy _____

4 cap/Silvia/Antonio _____

5 sandwiches/Maria _____

6 T-shirt/Antonio/John _____

Describing photographs

When we describe a photograph or a picture, we talk about what we see as if it is happening **now**. So we use the **present continuous** tense to describe what we see in a photograph or picture.

When you have a photograph or picture to describe, there are some things you can think about that will help you to say a lot about the picture. Ask yourself these questions:

Who is in the picture?
What are they doing?
What is happening around them?

> There are four children in the picture. They are playing football. The sun is shining. They are happy. They are having fun.

1 **Read, look and answer the questions.**

Alice is at home. She is talking on the phone to Antonio.

Antonio: Hi, Alice . What are you doing?

Alice: I'm sitting in the living room. My sister is watching TV. She's sitting in a big chair. My brother isn't watching TV. He's playing with his cars on the floor. My mum and dad are reading. We are all eating cake and drinking lemonade...

1 Is Alice talking to her mum? _____

2 Is Alice sitting in the bedroom? _____

3 Is her sister reading a book? _____

4 Is her sister sitting in the living room? _____

5 What is her brother doing? _____

6 Are her mum and dad watching TV? _____

7 Who is eating cake? _____

8 Are they drinking water? _____

2 **Look and write sentences.**

0   *He is reading a newspaper.*

1   _____

2   _____

3   _____

4   _____

5   _____

LESSON 5 *Test Yourself*

1 Put apostrophes in the correct places.

0   *It is Mike's party.*
1   Lets sit here.
2   Shes running round the track.
3   Theyre sitting in the hall.
4   Im having a great time.
5   Look at Annas hair!
6   Theres a volleyball game today.
7   There arent any clocks in here.

2 Complete the sentences with *some, any, a* and *an*.

0   She's got *some* chocolate and *a* sandwich.
1   She's got _____ new T-shirt but she hasn't got _____ socks.
2   She hasn't got _____ apple but she has got _____ oranges.
3   She's got _____ purple trainers.
4   She's got _____ elephant – it's a bag.
5   She hasn't got _____ books but she has got _____ magazines.

3 Put the words in the right order.

0   Carla writing a postcard is   *Carla is writing a postcard.*
1   having a time great I'm   _____
2   dog to is Claudia talking her   _____
3   me Excuse – sitting my you're in seat   _____
4   in They're sitting sun the   _____
5   looking Tom's for Roberto.   _____
6   are My playing friends basketball _____
7   friend my Daniel waiting I'm for   _____

4 **Complete the sentences using the correct form of these verbs.**

| listen   read   sit   watch   wear   ~~wear~~   write |

There is a computer on the wall. Silvia is on the right. She (0) *is wearing* a white shirt and

a pink top. She (1) _____ an e-mail.

Adam and Rosa are in the sports hall. Adam (2) _____ to music. Rosa is on the left.

Daniel (3) _____ a book. He (4) _____ a red T-shirt.

Maria (5) _____ television. She (6) _____ in a blue chair.

Her feet are on the table.

5 **Underline the correct answer.**

0 _____ cap is this?
   a. Who's   b. Who   c. <u>Whose</u>

1 _____ go to the party.
   a. Let   b. Let's   c. Lets

2 All the runners are _____ the stadium.
   a. in   b. on   c. here

3 Is that your camera _____ the chair?
   a. in   b. on   c. left

4 She's _____ nervous.
   a. feeling   b. feel   c. feels

5 They'_____ watching a programme.
   a. is   b. are   c. re

6 There _____ any windows in this room.
   a. aren't   b. are   c. 're

7 He's got _____ money.
   a. any   b. some   c. lots

4 ANIMALS

Can it talk?

Can

We also use **can** to talk about **abilities**.

Affirmative	Negative	Questions	Short answers
I can	I can't	Can I cook?	Yes, I can./No, I can't.
you can	you can't	Can you dance?	Yes, you can./No, you can't.
he can	he can't	Can he swim?	Yes, he can./No, he can't.
she can	she can't	Can she run?	Yes, she can./No, she can't.
it can	it can't	Can it fly?	Yes, it can./No, it can't.
we can	we can't	Can we write?	Yes, we can./No, we can't.
you can	you can't	Can you read?	Yes, you can./No, you can't.
they can	they can't	Can they sing?	Yes, they can./No, they can't.

Can has the same form for all persons so there are no endings to remember.

    I **can** dance.
    He **can** sing.
    She **can't** speak Italian.
    They **can** write English.

---

1 **Four students are talking about sport.
Read and answer the questions.**

Catherine
I love running. I can run very fast. I can jump too, but I can't swim.

Tony
I can't run very fast, but I can play football and I can swim.

Mark
I can play basketball – it's my favourite sport. I can't play football.

Emily
I don't like football. I can dance – I'm very good. But I can't run fast and I can't jump.

0   *Can* Catherine run fast?   *Yes, she can.*

1   _____ Tony play football?   _____

2   _____ Mark play football?   _____

3   _____ Emily run fast?   _____

4   _____ Catherine swim?   _____

5   _____ Mark play basketball?   _____

2 **Complete the sentences with these words.**

| ~~How old~~ What What Where Where Who Whose |

0   *How old* is Bonanza? She's two years old.
1   _____ is London? It's in England.
2   _____ colour is Smokey? He's grey.
3   _____ parrot is Cookie? He's Tom's.
4   _____ has got a dog called Daisy? Martin has.
5   _____ is Prince? He's in the garden.
6   _____ can Smokey do? He can climb trees.

3 **Write some funny questions. Ask a friend to answer them. Use some of these animals and verbs to help you.**

| budgie   cats   elephants   goldfish   horses   mice   parrots   rabbits
dance   jump   play football   sing   swim   talk   walk |

0   *Can elephants dance?*   *No, they can't.*   3   _____?
00 *Can parrots talk?*   *Yes, they can.*   _____
1   _____?   4   _____?
    _____   _____
2   _____?   5   _____?
    _____

4 **Complete the dialogue with these words.**

| can see   I can   I can't   What   What
Where   ~~Who~~   Who |

A: 0 *Who* can you see?
B: 1 I _____ a man and a woman.
A: 2 _____ are they doing?
B: They are sitting at a table.

A: Can you see a woman in a red top?
B: 3 Yes, _____ .
A: 4 _____ has she got?
B: She's got a green parrot.

A: 5 _____ is the grey bag?
B: It's on the table.
A: 6 _____ is holding the bag?
B: The man is holding the bag.

A: Can you see what's in the bag?
B: 7 No, I _____ .

5 **Put the words in the right order to make questions.**

0   animal Which fly can   *Which animal can fly?*
1   Who fast run can
    _____?
2   time it What is
    _____?
3   like you animal Which do
    _____?
4   do sleep goldfish How
    _____?
5   When eat do they
    _____?
6   this Whose is rabbit
    _____?
7   the How horse old is
    _____?
8   can see you What
    _____?
9   Where sleep mice do
    _____?

Is it drinking?

Present continuous: questions, short answers, negative

Let's look at the **present continuous** tense again to see how we make questions, short answers and negative sentences.

Remember – we use the **present continuous** to talk about what is happening **now**.

Questions	Short answers	Negative
Am I watching the race?	Yes, I am./No, I'm not.	I'm not watching the race.
Are you watching the race?	Yes, you are./No, you're not.	You're not watching the race.
Is he watching the race?	Yes, he is./No, he isn't.	He isn't watching the race.
Is she watching the race?	Yes, she is./No, she isn't.	She isn't watching the race.
Is it watching the race?	Yes, it is./No, it isn't.	It isn't watching the race.
Are we watching the race?	Yes, we are./No, we're not.	We're not watching the race.
Are you watching the race?	Yes, you are./No, you're not.	You're not watching the race.
Are they watching the race?	Yes, they are./No, they aren't.	They aren't watching the race.

For **short answers** you can choose which form to use.
You can use either
> **you're not / he's not**
>
> or
>
> **you aren't / he isn't**.

But you must use **I'm not** for the first person singular (we never say **I amn't**).

For short answers we just use the verb **be**. We don't repeat the main verb.
> Are you running? Yes, I **am**.
> Is Tim writing a letter? No, he **isn't**.

---

1 Look at the pictures and write answers.

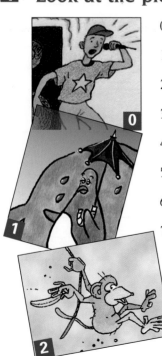

0	Is he singing?	*Yes, he is.*
1	Is it holding a mountain bike?	_____
2	Is it playing football?	_____
3	Are they smiling?	_____
4	Is it playing tennis?	_____
5	Is she standing?	_____
6	Are they dancing?	_____
7	Are they singing?	_____

2 Write questions.

| 0 | elephant/write an e-mail | *Is the elephant writing an e-mail?* |
| 00 | cats/swim in the sea | *Are the cats swimming in the sea?* |

1 tiger/dance _____?

2 lions/fight _____?

3 giraffe/sit _____?

4 mouse/run _____?

5 horse/eat a cake _____?

6 elephants/having a shower _____?

3 Look at exercise 2 again and write negative sentences.

0 *The elephant isn't writing an e-mail.*
00 *The cats aren't swimming in the sea.*

1 _____

2 _____

3 _____

4 _____

5 _____

6 _____

4 Complete the sentences with the correct form of the verb in brackets.

0 Today we *are having* a dancing competition at school with twenty boys and girls who are competitors. (have)

1 Is the competition _____ now? (start)

2 No, it isn't starting now. The competitors _____ ready now. (get)

3 Oh look! They are _____ out. (come)

4 Look! Marina _____ a cool dress – it's green and orange. (wear)

5 Oh no! What is Bill _____ ?
He looks very silly! (wear)

6 They _____ some nice music now. (play)

7 All the competitors _____ . (dance)

8 They look wonderful. Wait! What's Bill _____ ? (do)

9 He _____ . (not dance) He _____ ! (sing)

Is Tom shorter than Jerry?

1 Comparative adjectives: –er

We use **adjectives** when we want to say more about nouns or pronouns. We can, for example, talk about the colour, the shape, the amount, and the size of something, and we can give our opinion of it. Adjectives go before nouns and after the verb **be**.

> This **old** book.
> That girl is **nice**.

When we want to compare two things, we use the **comparative** form of the adjectives.

For many adjectives, we make the **comparative** form by adding **–er** to the end of the adjective.

> old – old**er**
> fast – fast**er**

But there are some rules for you to remember.

- For adjectives of one syllable that end in a vowel followed by a consonant (**big**, **fat**), we double the last consonant before adding **–er.**
  big – big**ger**
  fat – fat**ter**

- For adjectives that end in **e** (**large**, **nice**), we only add **–r.**
  large – large**r**
  nice – nice**r**

- For adjectives that end in **y** (funny, happy), we change the **y** to **i** and then add **–er.**
  funny – funn**ier**
  happy – happ**ier**

- There are also some irregular comparative adjectives. The two most common ones are
  good – **better**
  bad – **worse**

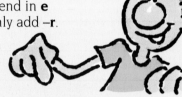

2 Than

When we compare two things or people and we use the **comparative** form, we also use **than** *after* the **comparative adjective**.

> Paul is taller **than** Alan.
> Your work is better **than** mine.

1 ## Tick the correct sentences.

0   My spelling is worse than Helen's.   ✓

1   Jim's writing is much gooder than Tom's.   ☐

2   My little sister thinks *Tom and Jerry* is funner than *Mickey Mouse*.   ☐

3   This elephant is much biger than that one.   ☐

4   Jim's hair is fairer than George's.   ☐

5   A lion is stronger than a dog.   ☐

6   Rabbits are largier than mice.   ☐

7   This CD is cool, but the new one is cooler!   ☐

8   Look at the giraffe. It's taller to the tree.   ☐

2 Write sentences using comparative adjectives.

0 Helen's dress is new.   *Maria's dress is newer.*

1 Claudia is clever.   Sissy _____

2 George is fast.   Silvia _____

3 They are happy.   We're _____

4 Antonio has got dark hair.   Bill _____

5 Spanish is easy.   English _____

6 Helena is young.   Maria _____

7 Your bar of chocolate is nice.   My cake _____

8 'Football Italia' is a good programme. 'Sport Today' _____

9 Marina is short.   Claudia _____

3 Write sentences comparing each pair of things. Use these adjectives to help you.

bad big difficult easy fast good nice old slow small young

0 elephant/mouse   *An elephant is stronger than a mouse.*

1 Britney Spears/Madonna   _____

2 English/Spanish   _____

3 bicycle/car   _____

4 village/city   _____

5 chocolate/ice cream   _____

4 Now make questions from your sentences and ask a friend.

0 *Is an elephant stronger than a mouse?*

1 _____

2 _____

3 _____

4 _____

5 _____

4 ANIMALS

LESSON 4 — *Use Your Grammar*

Postcards

When we are on holiday and send postcards to our friends, we usually say where we are and what we are doing – we say what is happening on our holiday. So, we use the **present continuous** tense when we write postcards.

Of course, you aren't on holiday at the moment – you are studying grammar! But you can use your imagination when you write postcards in the exercises in your book. You can imagine where you are and what you are doing. You can imagine who you are with, and who you are sending your postcard to.

1 **Read the postcard from Catherine to Nick.**

Dear Nick,
How are you? Are you having a nice time in Italy?
What are you doing there? Can you swim? I can't!
I'm not away on holiday this summer. I'm at home
and I'm playing with my friends. We're having fun!
Is Italy nicer than England?
Love,
Catherine

2 **Answer the questions.**

1   Where is Nick?   _____

2   Can Catherine swim?   _____

3   Is she away on holiday?   _____

4   Where is she staying?   _____

5   What is she doing?   _____

6   Who is having fun?   _____

3 Read Nick's answer to Catherine. Then complete the sentences with the correct form of the verbs in brackets.

Dear Catherine,
Thank you for your postcard.
I (O) *am having* (have) a great time in Italy.
We (1) _____ (visit) lots of old places and we
(2) _____ (see) beautiful cities. I (3) _____ (eat)
wonderful spaghetti – but I (4) _____ (not drink) any
wine! It's really nice here and I'm happy we (5) _____
(not come) home now.
See you soon,

Love
Nick

P.S. No, I can't swim!

4 Answer these questions using your imagination.

1 You are on holiday. Where are you? _____.

2 Are you having a good time?_____.

3 Are you staying in a hotel? _____.

4 What food are you eating? _____.

5 What are you doing there? _____.

6 Are you swimming? _____.

5 Now write a postcard to your friend telling him/her about your holiday.

_____

_____

_____

_____

_____

_____

Test Yourself

1 **Put apostrophes in the correct places.**

0   George *can't* run today – he is tired.

1   Im not coming on holiday with you.

2   Catherine isnt in the hall.

3   They arent playing with us.

4   Hes having a party today.

5   He cant touch his toes.

2 **Make questions from the sentences in exercise 1.**

0   *Can George run today?*

1   _____ ?

2   _____ ?

3   _____ ?

4   _____ ?

5   _____ ?

3 **Sarah is talking to a new girl at school. Complete the dialogue with these words.**

| How old   what   where   ~~when~~   who   whose |

Hi Elena.

Sarah: Look at all the children in the classroom.

Elena: (0) *When* does the lesson start?
Sarah: It starts at six o'clock.

Elena: (1) _____ is that girl eating the apple?
Sarah: Oh, that's Sofia.

Hi Sarah.

Elena: (2) _____ is she?
Sarah: She's eleven.

Elena: (3) And _____ chair is this?
Sarah: This is Jim's chair – and that one is mine.

Elena: (4) _____ does the teacher sit?
Sarah: She sits over there.

Elena: (5) _____ is that?
Sarah: It's a bar of chocolate. It's a present for Miss Kathy.

4 **Underline the correct answer.**

0	Are you eating?	a. <u>Yes, I am.</u>	b. Yes, I'm.	c. Yes, I are.
1	Can she sing?	a. Yes, she is.	b. Yes, she can.	c. She can't.
2	How old is Susan?	a. She's a girl.	b. Yes, she is.	c. She's ten.
3	Is Marianna taller than Clauda?	a. Yes, she's.	b. Yes, she does.	c. Yes, she is.
4	Can you see him?	a. No, I can't.	b. No, I can.	c. No, I'm not.
5	Where is Anna?	a. She's in the car.	b. She here.	c. No, she isn't.
6	Can they swim?	a. No, they can't.	b. No, they aren't.	c. No, they don't.
7	What is this?	a. It isn't.	b. It's a pen.	c. Is this a pen.
8	Is Bill coming today?	a. No, he is.	b. No, he doesn't.	c. No, he isn't.
9	Whose book is this?	a. It's Tom.	b. It's Tom's.	c. No, it isn't.

5 **Look at the chart and complete the sentences
with the correct forms of** *fast, good, tall, old.*

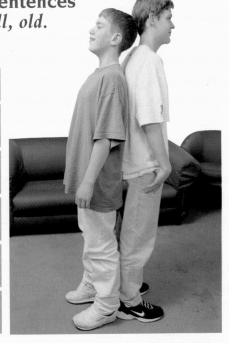

	Jim	Sam	Jane
Age	10	9	11
Height	1.5m	1.6m	1.7m
Swimming	**	*	X
Volleyball	*	**	**

Key: *=good   **=very good

Jim is ten. Jim is (0) *older* than Sam, but he isn't very tall. Sam is (1) _____ than Jim.

Jane is taller than Sam and Jim, and she is (2) _____ than them, too.

Sam and Jim can swim, but Jane can't. They can all play volleyball, but Sam and Jane are (3)

_____ than Jim.

What time do you get up?

---

❶ Prepositions of time: *at, in, from ... to*

We use **in** before months:
  in February
  in June.
  in October.

We use **in** before parts of the day:
  in the morning
  in the afternoon
  in the evening

But note:
  at night

We use **at** with times:
  at six o'clock
  at a quarter to ten.
  at twenty five past seven
  at midday
  at noon
  at midnight

We use **from** and **to** to show the period of time from when something starts to when it finishes.

  from Monday **to** Friday
  from May **to** June
  From four o'clock **to** half past five

❷ Present simple: routines

We can use the **present simple** tense to talk about routines. These are habits or things which happen again and again.
  I get up at eight o'clock.
  I go to school.
  She doesn't have a shower every morning.
  Do you start lessons at nine o'clock?

❸ *Usually*

We often use **usually** with verbs in the **present simple**.

  He **usually** brushes his teeth in the morning.
  What time do you **usually** have dinner?

> **Top Tip!**
> The word **usually** goes before the main verb in the sentence.
>   He **usually** brushes his teeth in the morning.
>   What time do you **usually** have dinner?

---

❶ Catherine and John are at Summer Camp. Complete the dialogue with *at, in, from ... to*.

Monday	
9.00 - 10.00	swimming
10.00 - 12.00	gymnastics
12.00 - 1.00	lunch
1.00 - 2.00	basketball
2.00 - 3.00	tennis

Catherine: What have we got today?
John: (0) *At* nine o'clock we've got swimming.
Catherine: Have we got volleyball today?
John: No, it's tomorrow.
Catherine: What time is gymnastics?
John: (1) _____ ten o'clock _____ twelve o'clock.
Catherine: What time's lunch?
John: (2) _____ twelve o'clock of course!
Catherine: (3) What have we got _____ the afternoon?
John: Basketball and tennis.
Catherine: (4) Is tennis _____ one o'clock?
John: (5) No, it's _____ two o'clock.

2 Andy's family does everything at the wrong time. Write questions.

0   Andy's dad/get up
What time does Andy's dad get up?

1   Andy's mum/go to work

_____ ?

2   The baby and Andy/have breakfast

_____ ?

3   Sam the dog/go to school

_____ ?

4   The baby/go to bed

_____ ?

5   Andy's brother/do homework

_____ ?

3 Now write the answers.

0   Andy's dad/get up/midnight
Andy's dad gets up at midnight.

1   Andy's mum/go to work/midday

_____

2   The baby and Andy/have breakfast/five

_____

3   Sam the dog/go to school/the evening

_____

4   The baby/go to bed/ten o'clock/the morning

_____

5   Andy's brother/do homework/midnight

_____

4 Write five sentences about what you usually do every day.

1   _____

2   _____

3   _____

4   _____

5   _____

LESSON 2 *I'm looking at the stars*

We use the **present simple** to talk about what we **usually** do, and the **present continuous** to talk about what we are doing **now**.

>   I **do** my homework every afternoon. (usually, every day)
>   I'**m doing** my homework. (now, at the moment)

If you aren't sure whether to use the **present simple** or the **present continuous**, think about **when** – is it something that's happening **now/at the moment** or something that **usually/regularly** happens?

>   I **am reading** this book **now**.
>   I **usually read** school books in the afternoon.

When you see the words **now** or **at the moment** in a sentence expect to find the **present continuous**.
When you see the words **usually** or **every** in a sentence expect to find the **present simple**.

>   The children **are playing** football **at the moment**.
>   Mum and dad **watch** television **every evening**.

Top Tip!
We can use both the **present simple** and the **present continuous** in the same sentence when we are comparing things we **usually** do with things we are doing **now**.

>   I **usually** eat eggs for breakfast, but **today** I am eating chocolate cake!

---

1 **Read Astrid's letter to her friend Angie. Then complete the sentences with the present simple or the present continuous.**

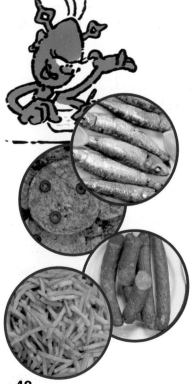

Dear Angie,

Today is Monday and I (0) *am* (be) very happy. It's very cold and

I (1) _____ (sit) by the swimming pool. It is six o'clock in the

evening and I (2) _____ (have) breakfast. Of course,

I usually (3) _____ (have) breakfast at midnight.

Today I (4) _____ (eat) chocolate cake and ice cream but

I usually (5) _____ (eat) pizza and chips. I usually (6) _____

(drink) coke for breakfast but today I (7) _____ (have) water. I can

hear music – someone (8) _____ (play) a new CD. It's wonderful – I

(9) _____ (like) that band.

Hope you are well.

Love,

Astrid

2 Look at Angie's letter to Astrid and underline the mistakes. Then correct them.

Dear Astrid,

Today <u>is being</u> Wednesday and I is very cool! I listen to Ricky Martin's new CD

_____ is _____

– it's wonderful and I'm liking it a lot. At the moment I have breakfast, too but I don't drink water

_____

and I don't eat chocolate cake. I'm hating chocolate cake! My favourite is fish cake!

_____

I usually am having lunch at midnight.

_____

Love,
Angie

3 Write questions and answers about Astrid and Arnie.

0   Astrid/gymnastics/midnight
    Does Astrid do gymnastics at midnight?   ✓
    Yes, she does.

1   Astrid and Arnie/start work/9 o'clock   ✗

    _____ ?

    _____

2   Arnie/go swimming/winter   ✓

    _____ ?

    _____

3   Astrid and Arnie/run in the park/morning   ✗

    _____ ?

    _____

4   Arnie/eat sandwiches/lunchtime   ✗

    _____ ?

    _____

5   Astrid/eat chocolate cake/breakfast   ✓

    _____ ?

    _____

4 Write questions and answers from the words below.

0   rain/now   December
    Is it raining now?
    No, it isn't raining now, but it usually rains in December.

1   Marina/play tennis/at the moment   Tuesday

    _____ ?

    No, _____

2   You/watch/television/now   in the evening

    _____ ?

    No, _____

3   the boys/play volleyball/now   Saturday

    _____ ?

    No, _____

4   the sun/shine/at the moment   June

    _____ ?

    No, _____

5   we go/Italian restaurant/tonight   Friday

    _____ ?

    No, _____

5 TIME AND SPACE

Are there any computers?

---

1 Is/Are there ...? + short answers

We make the question form by putting is/are before **there**: **Is there ...?/Are there ...?**
We can use **There is/There are** to make affirmative or negative answers.

Questions	Short answers	Full answers
Is there a computer?	Yes, there is.	Yes, there is a computer.
Is there a table?	No, there isn't.	No, there isn't a table.
Are there any chairs?	Yes, there are.	Yes, there are some chairs.
Are there any windows?	No, there aren't.	No, there aren't any windows.

2 How many ...?

We use **How many ...?** to ask about the number of things or people. After **How many ...?** we use plural nouns.

> **How many** computers are there? There are **five** computers.
> **How many** beds are there in this room? **None.**

3 Prepositions of place: *next to, near, opposite*

We use **next to** when something or somebody is by the side of something/somebody else.
> My house is **next to** Mary's house.
> Alice is sitting **next to** Penny.

We use **near** when something or somebody is close to something/somebody else.
> The chair is **near** the table.
> Our house is **near** to my school.

We use **opposite** when something or somebody is facing something/somebody else but there is some space between them.
> The shoe shop is **opposite** the cinema in Green Street.
> My desk is **opposite** the blackboard.

---

1 Complete the sentences with *Is there* or *Are there*.
Then answer the questions with short answers.

0   *Is there* a pen on the table? ✓   *Yes, there is.*

1   _____ any chocolates in the bag? ✓   _____

2   _____ any books in your room? ✗   _____

3   _____ a cartoon on television? ✗   _____

4   _____ any people in the stadium? ✓   _____

5   _____ an elephant in the zoo? ✗   _____

6   _____ a photograph on the wall? ✓   _____

7   _____ any crocodiles in the water? ✗   _____

2 How many animals are there in the jungle?

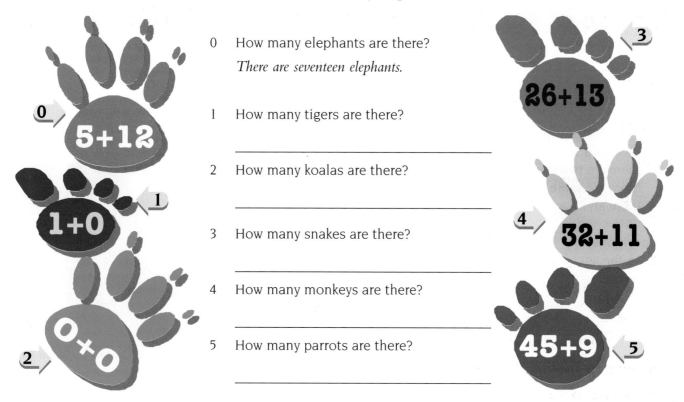

0 How many elephants are there?
There are seventeen elephants.

1 How many tigers are there?

_____

2 How many koalas are there?

_____

3 How many snakes are there?

_____

4 How many monkeys are there?

_____

5 How many parrots are there?

_____

3 Write questions using *Where is* or *Where are*. Then look at the map of the zoo and write answers with *next to, near* or *opposite*.

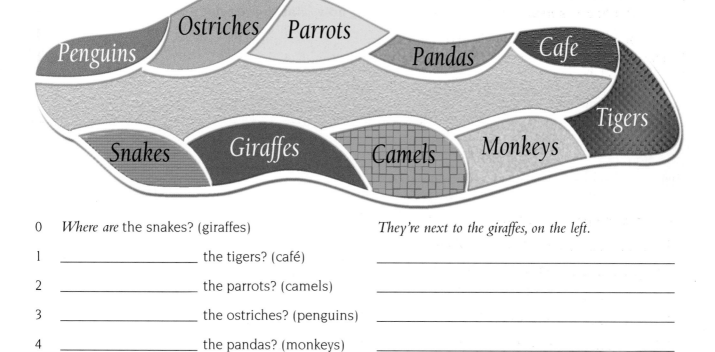

0 *Where are* the snakes? (giraffes)   *They're next to the giraffes, on the left.*

1 _____ the tigers? (café)   _____

2 _____ the parrots? (camels)   _____

3 _____ the ostriches? (penguins)   _____

4 _____ the pandas? (monkeys)   _____

5 _____ the penguins? (snakes)   _____

6 _____ the giraffes? (camels)   _____

7 _____ the café? (pandas)   _____

LESSON 4 *Use Your Grammar*

1 Describing a place

Think –

Think about **what** things there are in your town, your house, your room. Make a list, putting the most important things at the top and the least important things at the bottom of your list.

There is **a** sports centre in my city.

There are **two** swimming pools.

There are **some** parks.

There aren't **any** tennis courts or information centres.

Prepositions help you to say exactly **where** the things are.

on the left

on the right

next to

near

opposite

2 Your daily routine

Remember to use the **present simple** when you write or talk about things you do regularly. The word **usually** and phrases using the word **every** are very useful when you make sentences about routines.

3 What are you doing now?

What are you doing at the moment? Are you reading? Are you eating ice cream now?

When we talk or write about things that are happening **now** or **at the moment**, we use the **present continuous** tense.

Think –

Think about what is happening around you at the moment. Describe what's happening using the **present continuous.**

1 Read and answer the questions.

Today Astrid and Arnie are having a picnic on the beach.

They usually have a picnic on Saturdays in the summer.

They usually take chocolate and banana sandwiches and cold water.

Arnie is swimming but Astrid is sitting on the beach and drinking.

She is very hot.

Today there aren't any people on the beach ... but there are some aliens!

1 Where are Astrid and Arnie? _____

2 What are they doing? _____

3 Do they usually have a picnic on Sundays? _____

4 What do they usually take with them to eat? _____

5 Is Arnie sitting on the beach? _____

6 Is Astrid hot? _____

7 What is she doing? _____

8 Are there any people on the beach? _____

9 Are there any aliens on the beach? _____

2 **Read about Stella Nova.**

My planet.
**Stella Nova is a beautiful small planet. I live in Alien City. There is a
big park with lots of red trees and blue flowers.
My house is next to the park and there are two swimming pools.
There aren't any banks. We don't use money but we have small
diamonds. There is one very big supermarket between the
swimming pools, but there aren't any small shops. You can buy
everything at the supermarket – with diamonds of course!**

3 **Write about your village, town or city. Use the following words from
this unit.**

in   opposite   next to   on the left/right   near   there is   there are

4 **Answer these questions about your bedroom. Use some of the words
from this unit.**

1 What is opposite the window in your bedroom? _____

2 Where is your bed? _____

3 What is near your bed? _____

4 Are there any books in your bedroom? _____

5 Is there a TV in your bedroom? _____

6 What is near the door in your bedroom? _____

7 Is there a table in your bedroom? _____

8 Is there a chair next to your bed? _____

LESSON 5 Test Yourself

1 Look at the map and complete the sentences with the correct form of *there is / there are*, and prepositions of place.

INFORMATION OFFICE	RESTAURANT	STATION	CINEMA	PARK HOTEL	PARK	SCHOOL

SUPER MARKET	CAFÉ	BOOKSHOP	BANK	METROPOL HOTEL	SPORTS SHOP	CAR PARK

A: Excuse me. (0) *Is there* a hotel here, please?

B: Yes, (1) _____ two hotels. The Metropol Hotel is on the (2) _____, next to the bank. The Park Hotel is (3) _____ the Metropol Hotel – it's (4) _____ the park.

A: Thank you. Where can I buy a drink?

B: You can buy a drink at the café. It's on your (5) _____, next to the bookshop. (6) _____ a restaurant opposite the café, too.

A: Great! (7) _____ an Information Office here?

B: Yes. It's on your left, (8) _____ the restaurant.

A: Thank you very much.

A: Oh – (9) _____ any discos in this town?

B: No, sorry. (10) _____ any discos here.

2 Look at the map again and write answers.

0 Is there a cinema?   *Yes, there is.*

1 Is there a Post Office?   _____

2 Are there any hotels?   _____

3 Is there a park?   _____

4 Are there any houses?   _____

5 Are there any shops?   _____

3 Complete the sentences with these words.

~~How many~~   What   What time   When   Where are   Where is

0   *How many* aliens are there on the moon?

1   _____ is the astronaut doing now?

2   _____ the fridge?

3   _____ the computers?

4   _____ do you have a shower? At half past seven.

5   _____ does he play the guitar? In the evening.

4 Complete the sentences with the correct form of the verb in brackets.

0   I *am reading* a letter from my penfriend. (read)

1   I _____ to my penfriend every week. (write)

2   My sister usually _____ to her penfriend every month. (write)

3   She usually _____ to her boyfriend on the telephone every day. (speak)

4   She _____ to him now. (talk)

5 Underline the correct word(s).

0   There aren't **any/some** shops in our village.

1   Where **is/are** my new jeans?

2   How many children are there? **None/Not any.**

3   Is there an alien in our school? Yes, **there's/there is!**

4   I live **next/near** the park.

5   Maria sits **at/on** my left.

6   There is a dog **in/on** the middle of our classroom!

7   Are there **some/any** chocolates in your bag?

8   I usually go for a walk **in/at** the afternoon.

9   We are **watching/watch** a football match now.

6 FREE TIME

LESSON 1 — *What would you like?*

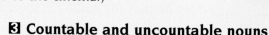

1 Would like + noun/infinitive

We use the phrase **would like** to ask for things politely or to say **what we want to do**. The short form is **'d like.**

We use **would like** with a noun.
   I **would like** a pizza. (I**'d like** a pizza.)
   I **would like** some milk. (I**'d like** some milk.)

We use **would like** with the infinitive form of the verb (to see, to go, to play, etc).
   I **would like** to eat some chocolate. (I**'d like** to eat some chocolate.)
   I **would like** to go to the cinema. (I**'d like** to go to the cinema.)

2 that/those/this/these

We use **that** and **those** for people or things that aren't near us.
We use **that** to talk about **one** thing or person.
   Look at **that** car.

We use **those** to talk about **plurals**.
   What are **those** children doing?

We use **this** and **these** with people or things that are near us.
We use **this** for **one** thing or person.
   Do you want **this** cake?

We use **these** for **plurals**.
   These are my books.

3 Countable and uncountable nouns

We make the plurals for lots of nouns by adding –**s**: they are **countable nouns**.
   one book two book**s**
   one dog   three dog**s**

But some nouns **don't** have a plural form. These nouns are called **uncountable nouns**.
   cheese, milk, meat, coffee

With **uncountable nouns** we don't use the infinitive article (a/an). Instead, we can use **some**.
   I would like **some** coffee

---

1 **Complete the dialogue with *would like + some / a / to.***

John: (0) Cool! Look at that bike. I*'d like* a bike for Christmas.

Paul: (1) I _____ new CDs.

Marianna: (2) I _____ small television

             for my bedroom.

Catherine: Well, I think you're all very greedy.

Marianna: (3) Why? What _____ ,

             Catherine?

Catherine: (4) I _____ win my next race.

2 **Look and write questions and answers.**

0   *What would* Helen *like?*
    (j) *She'd like some cheese.*

1   _____ Antonio _____ ?
    (e) _____

2   _____ Marina _____ ?
    (f) _____

3   _____ George _____ ?
    (d) _____

4   _____ Marianna _____ ?
    (g) _____

5   _____ Bill _____ ?
    (b) _____

6   _____ Sissy _____ ?
    (i) _____

7   _____ Jim _____ ?
    (h) _____

3 **Complete with *this, that, these* or *those*.**

Martin: The food looks delicious. What would you like, Anna?

Anna: One of (1) _____ pizzas over there by the fruit, please.

Martin: Don't you want (2) _____ pizza here?

Anna: No thanks, I don't like sausage on pizza. And I'd like some of (3) _____ salad that Kathy's eating.

Martin: Would you like some of (4) _____ chips over there? They look good.

Anna: No thanks. Are (5) _____ our knives and forks here?

Martin: Yes, they are. But don't eat them!

Anna: (6) _____'s not funny! I'm very hungry but I can't eat metal. I'm not Michel Lotito!

LESSON 2 *Are you good at dancing?*

1 –ing

We form the gerund by adding the ending **–ing** to the verb. Gerunds are like nouns.

Verb	Gerund
listen	listening
play	playing
sing	singing
swim	swimming
run	running

2 *like, love, hate + –ing*

When we want to talk about what things we like or don't like doing, we can use these verbs and the **gerund**.

> I like **swimming**.
> Bob and Ben hate **dancing**.
> Do you like **reading**?

3 *good at + –ing*

When we want to talk about something we do well, we can use the phrase **good at**.
We can use **good at** before a gerund or before a noun.

> I'm **good at** running.
> Are you **good at** tennis?

---

1 Complete the dialogue.

Claudia: (0) Do you *like* sport?

Helen: (1) Well, I like swimming and I love running, but I'm not very good _____ them.

(2) I like _____ them on television.

Claudia: (3) Are you _____ at dancing?

Helen: (4) No, I hate dancing. I don't _____ music.

Claudia: (5) _____ are you good at?

Helen: (6) I'm _____ at computer games ... and I love sleeping!

2 Complete the sentences with the correct form of these verbs.

dance   hate   ~~like~~   like   love   not be   play

0   Helen *likes* swimming.

1   She _____ running.

2   She _____ very good at them.

3   She's very good at _____ computer games.

4   She isn't good at _____ . She doesn't like it.

5   She _____ music.

6   She _____ watching swimming and running on television.

3 Write questions and short answers about Helen.

0   like/swimming?   *Does Helen like swimming?*   *Yes, she does.*

1   like/running?   _____

2   good at/swimming/running?   _____

3   good at/dancing?   _____

4   like/music?   _____

5   good at/computer games?   _____

4 Answer the questions.

1   Do you like watching TV?

    _____

2   Does your friend like going to the cinema?

    _____

3   Is your friend good at playing volleyball?

    _____

4   Does your teacher like cake?

    _____

5   Do you love chocolate?

    _____

6   Are you good at swimming?

    _____

5 Write the words in the correct box.

~~book~~
cinema
dancing
letter
like
listen
music
play
reading
sing
singing
song
writing

VERB	NOUN
	book

GERUND

LESSON 3 — *Which one do you want?*

1 Comparative adjectives: *more* + adjective

We make the **comparative** form of one-syllable adjectives by adding **–er**:
longer smaller.

We form the comparative of adjectives with two or more syllables by putting **more** before the adjective.
beautiful – **more** beautiful
interesting – **more** interesting
difficult – **more** difficult

Note – we still use **than** after the adjective.
My sister is more beautiful **than** me.

2 *How much is it?*

We use this phrase when we want to find out the price of something.
Usually, the answer we get will begin with **It's …** and then the price.
How much is this CD?
It's £14.
How much is that jacket?
It's only £20.

3 *Which one?*

We ask **Which one?** to find out what a person is going to choose.
Look at those wonderful T-shirts.
Which one do you want?
I'd like the blue **one**.

Here are some cakes.
Which one does Sally want?
She wants the chocolate **one**.

1 Tick the correct sentences.

0   A bag is more useful than a CD.   ✔

1   A snake is more long than a fish.   ☐

2   A parrot is beautifuller than a monkey.   ☐

3   Sports programmes are interestinger
    than cartoons.   ☐

4   The gold dress is more beautiful than the
    red one.   ☐

5   Kelly is taller than Rachel.   ☐

6   Basketball is excitinger than football.   ☐

7   Polish is more difficult than Italian.   ☐

2 Write the words in the correct box.

difficult ~~elephant~~ exciting look lovely picture speak start
table terrible think tree T-shirt wear wonderful

VERB	NOUN	ADJECTIVE
	elephant	

3 Use the words in exercise 2 to make funny sentences.

0 *The lovely elephant is sitting on the table.*

1 _____

2 _____

3 _____

4 _____

4 Write your own sentences.

1 _____ is more boring than _____

2 _____ is more interesting than _____

3 _____ is more beautiful than _____

4 _____ is more exciting than _____

5 Write questions and answers.

How much

blue dress/white top/big pizza/hamburger/CD player/video
£10.59 / £2.50 / £6.34 / £9.27 / £63.00 / £12.78

Question	**Answer**
0 *How much is the blue dress?*	*It's £10.59*
1 _____	_____
2 _____	_____
3 _____	_____
4 _____	_____
5 _____	_____

LESSON 4 *Use Your Grammar*

Interests and habits

When we are describing ourselves, our friends or family, or somebody famous, we can write about interests and habits.

To write about interests you can use verbs **like**, **love**, **hate** and the **gerund** or a **noun**.

> He **hates** skiing. I **love** tennis.
> I like **eating** in restaurants. I **like** ice cream.
> She **loves** studying grammar! I **hate** lessons!

And to write about habits you use the **present simple** tense.

Remember – when you are writing about what a person is **good at** or **not good at** you use **gerunds** or a **noun**.

> Mary is **good at** sport.
> Peter is **good at** playing football.
> I am really **bad at** writing compositions.
> She is **bad at** geography.

1 **Read about Claudia's brothers and sisters.**

My Family

I've got a big family – two brothers and two sisters and we live in a small town near Paris.

Bill is five years old. He loves eating big chocolate bars but he hates having a shower every day. Lucy is only two years old but she loves water. She likes having her shower and she loves the sea but she can't swim. Alice is ten. She's good at French and English and she's cleverer than me, but she doesn't like doing her homework. George loves eating hamburgers and chips with his friends. He's not good at school and hates all his lessons. He only likes food and girls. He's sixteen!

2 **Now answer the questions.**

1 Has Claudia got a small family? _____

2 Where does she live? _____

3 Has she got two brothers? _____

4 How old is Alice? _____

5 What is she good at? _____

6 What does George like doing? _____

7 Is he good at school? _____

8 What does Bill hate? _____

9 Is Claudia cleverer than Alice? _____

10 What does Lucy love? _____

3 **Complete the text with words from the box.**

better is good at lives more playing than

My friend Carl

My friend Carl (1) _____ in Rio. He's got a big family. He's got three brothers and four sisters.
Carl (2) _____ fifteen years old. He likes (3) _____ a lot of sports and he is really (4) _____
at football, volleyball, and tennis. The only sport he is bad (5) _____ is golf. He hates golf.
I'm (6) _____ at golf than Carl is.
Carl is a good student. He loves maths and he thinks it's (7) _____ interesting than any other lesson.
I don't think so. I think maths is more difficult (8) _____ geography or physics. My friend Carl is
cleverer than me.

4 **Answer the questions about yourself. Use complete sentences.**

1 What are you good at?

_____

2 What do you like to eat?

_____

3 Which lesson is more interesting – maths or english?

_____

4 What do you hate doing?

_____

LESSON 5 *Test Yourself*

1 Tick the correct sentences.

0 I like eggs. ☑

1 Football is boring than basketball. ☐

2 How many sandwich have we got? ☐

3 Don't to shout in the classroom. ☐

4 This T-shirt is nicer than that one. ☐

5 Lets go to the park. ☐

6 Please sitting down. ☐

2 Complete the sentences with *a/an*, *some* or *any*.

0 I'd like *some* bread.

1 Can I have _____ apple?

2 Would you like _____ bananas?

3 Please can I have _____ fruit?

4 Have you got _____ cakes?

5 I haven't got _____ ice cream.

3 Underline the correct word.

0 **Are/Is** there any sugar in my coffee?

1 There **is/are** lots of bread on the table.

2 There **is/are** some spaghetti in the cupboard.

3 **Are/Is** there any apples on the tree?

4 **Is/Are** there any children in the swimming pool?

5 There **are/is** lots of diamonds on Hula Hula.

4 **Look at exercise 3 and make the sentences negative.**

0   *There isn't any sugar in my coffee.*

1   _____

2   _____

3   _____

4   _____

5   _____

5 **Angie the Alien is visiting your house. Complete the dialogue with these words.**

| Can Do one than that ~~this~~ those Would |

Angie: (0) What's *this*?

You: It's my house.

Angie: (1) What's _____?

You: (2) It's a bottle. _____ you like a drink of water?

Angie: Yes, please. Yuk! It's terrible!

You: (3) _____ you want some cola?

Angie: (4) Yes, please. Cola is nicer _____ water. (5) What are _____ ?

You: Those are chocolates.

Angie: (6) _____ I have one?

You: Of course.

Angie: Yummy!

You: (7) Which _____ do you like?

Angie: All of them!

This was a Roman town

---

1 Past simple *to be*: *was, were*

Affirmative	Negative	Contractions	Questions	Short answers
I was	I was not	I wasn't	Was I?	Yes, I was./No, I wasn't.
you were	you were not	you weren't	Were you?	Yes, you were./No, you weren't.
he was	he was not	he wasn't	Was he?	Yes, he was./No, he wasn't.
she was	she was not	she wasn't	Was she?	Yes, she was./No, she wasn't.
it was	it was not	it wasn't	Was it?	Yes, it was./No, it wasn't.
we were	we were not	we weren't	Were we?	Yes, we were./No, we weren't.
you were	you were not	you weren't	Were you?	Yes, you were./No, you weren't.
they were	they were not	they weren't	Were they?	Yes, they were./No, they weren't.

Top Tip!
Remember to use **was** for the first and third person singular (I/he/she/it).

2 Prepositions of time: *ago*

Note that the preposition **ago** comes after the period of time.
three years **ago**
I was in London one month **ago**.
We were on holiday two weeks **ago**.

3 *There was/There were*

We can use **There was/There were** to talk about things that existed in the past.
There was a mouse in the kitchen yesterday.
There were lots of people at the theatre.

---

1 **Complete the sentences with** *was* **or** *were*.

0a I *was* at school.

0b My friend and I   : *We were at school.*

1a You _____ at the bank.

1b You and your friend : _____

2a Tania _____ at home.

2b Tania and her friend : _____

3a Jim _____ at the cinema.

3b Jim and his friend   : _____

4a The dog _____ in the garden.

4b The dog and the cat : _____

2 Anna is looking in the sports cupboard at the Games Village. Complete the sentences with *there was/were* and *there is/are*.

0	Yesterday *there were six* tennis rackets. (6)	Now *there are two.* (2)
1	Yesterday _____ mountain bikes. (3)	Now _____ (1)
2	Yesterday _____ basketball. (1)	Now _____ (4)
3	Yesterday _____ rollerblades. (2)	Now _____ (3)
4	Yesterday _____ tracksuit. (1)	Now _____ (2)
5	Yesterday _____ footballs. (10)	Now _____ (0)

3 Now answer the questions about yesterday.

0	Were there six tennis rackets?	*Yes, there were.*
1	Was there one basketball?	_____
2	Were there three rollerblades?	_____
3	Were there two tracksuits?	_____
4	Was there one football?	_____
5	Were there two mountain bikes?	_____

4 Put the words in the right order.

0	George was the cinema at last night	*George was at the cinema last night.*
1	was Anna the theatre at two weeks ago	_____
2	yesterday at school Bill was	_____
3	a month ago Helen and Jim in London were	_____
4	at home Jim three days ago was	_____
5	Marianna last week was in Rome	_____
6	I in America a year ago was	_____
7	Marina and Nick last weekend were at the beach	_____

7 A LONG TIME AGO

Life in Pompeii ended

Past simple: regular verbs: affirmative

It's very easy to form the **past simple** for regular verbs. All we do is add the ending **–ed** to the main verb.

Affirmative
I listen**ed**
you listen**ed**
he listen**ed**
she listen**ed**
it listen**ed**
we listen**ed**
you listen**ed**
they listen**ed**

There are a few easy rules to remember about spelling.
For verbs of one syllable that end with a **vowel** and a **consonant**, we double the last consonant before we add **–ed**.
   stop – stop**ped**

For verbs that end in e, we only add **–d**
to make the **past simple**.
   dance – dance**d**

For verbs that end in a **consonant** and
y, we take away the **y** and add **–ied**.
   study – stud**ied**

We use the **past simple** tense for a completed action in the past and to talk about what happened at a **specific/exact** time in the past – for example, something that happened **yesterday**, **two hours ago**, **seven hundred and thirty-four years ago, last Monday**.
   Harry **played** basketball **last Saturday**.
   I **studied** all day **yesterday**.

---

1 **Put these verbs into the past.**

0	look	*looked*
1	stay	_____
2	live	_____
3	stop	_____
4	close	_____
5	carry	_____
6	watch	_____
7	fit	_____

2 **Now try these.**

0	laugh	*laughed*
1	dance	_____
2	race	_____
3	ask	_____
4	cry	_____
5	discover	_____
6	believe	_____
7	jump	_____

3 Complete the text with the correct form of these verbs.

ask dance enjoy jump phone stay stop watch want

Astrid and Arnie were in town last night at a party. Arnie (0) *asked* Astrid to dance. Arnie's dancing was very

funny – he (1) _____ up and down and looked very silly!

The music was fabulous so they (2) _____ for a long time. After two hours they were really hot

and Astrid (3) _____ a pink drink, so they (4) _____ dancing.

Lots of their friends were at the party and they (5) _____ it so much that they (6) _____

there all night! In the morning, they (7) _____ the sun come up. They were so tired that they

(8) _____ for a taxi to take them home.

4 Underline the mistakes and then correct them.

0   The party <u>startted</u> at nine o'clock.   *started*

1   Dance music fillied the air.   _____

2   Everybody laughd at Arnie's funny dance.   _____

3   Astrid likd the pink drinks.   _____

4   They talkd to their friends.   _____

5   Astrid lovd the party.   _____

6   The party endid in the morning.   _____

5 Write about yourself. Use *yesterday, a week/year ago, last week/month* etc.

		what	**when**
0	watch	*I watched a sports programme on TV last night.*	
1	visit	_____	
2	like	_____	
3	hate	_____	
4	dance	_____	
5	walk	_____	
6	listen	_____	

7 A LONG TIME AGO

LESSON 3 · Did you watch TV?

Past simple: regular verbs: negative, questions and short answers

We form **past simple questions** and **negatives**, with the past simple of the auxilary verb **do did**.

Negative	Contractions	Questions	Short answers
I did not listen	I didn't listen	Did I listen?	Yes, I Did./No, I didn't.
you did not listen	you didn't listen	Did you listen?	Yes, you Did./No, you didn't.
he did not listen	he didn't listen	Did he listen?	Yes, he Did./No, he didn't.
she did not listen	she didn't listen	Did she listen?	Yes, she Did./No, she didn't.
it did not listen	it didn't listen	Did it listen?	Yes, it Did./No, it didn't.
we did not listen	we didn't listen	Did we listen?	Yes, we Did./No, we didn't.
you did not listen	you didn't listen	Did you listen?	Yes, you Did./No, you didn't.
they did not listen	they didn't listen	Did they listen?	Yes, they Did./No, they didn't.

Top Tip! Three important things to remember –
- We don't use the ending **–ed** for the negative or for questions in the past simple.
- We use **did** and **did not (didn't)** for negatives and questions in the past simple.
- We change the **word order** for questions.

---

1 **Sue is interviewing Carla and Roberto. Write questions.**

Questions for Roberto:

0   phone home/yesterday   ☑   *Did you phone home yesterday?*

1   talk/to your mum and dad   ☑   _____?

2   watch/the film last night   ☒   _____?

3   listen/your new CD   ☑   _____?

Questions for Carla:

4   enjoy/the party last week   ☑   _____?

5   like/the music   ☑   _____?

6   dance/a lot   ☒   _____?

7   stay/until midnight   ☒   _____?

2 **Put the words in the right order to make questions about Roberto and Carla. Then look at exercise 1 and write short answers.**

0   he Did yesterday phone home ?   *Did he phone home yesterday?*   *Yes, he did.*

1   mum and dad talk to Did he his ?   _____   _____

2   Did the film watch he last night ?   _____   _____

3   new CD his listen to he Did ?   _____   _____

4   last week she Did the party enjoy ?   _____   _____

5   like Did she the music ?   _____   _____

6   dance she Did a lot ?   _____   _____

7   midnight she stay until Did ?   _____   _____

3 **Underline the correct word(s).**

0   Tom **play tennis/<u>played tennis</u>** every day.

1   Marianna **works/worked** yesterday.

2   Helen felt sad when she **watches/watched** a sad film last night.

3   Marina **wants/wanted** her dinner now.

4   George **discovers/discovered** a strange animal in our garden yesterday.

5   Mum and Dad **phone/phoned** each other every day.

6   I **visit/visited** my grandmother a week ago.

7   I **hate/hated** that film on TV yesterday.

8   Anna and Mario **live/lived** in Italy a year ago.

9   Marianna **stays/stayed** at her friend's house last night.

4 **Write questions. Use your own words, too.**

0   watch/last night   *Did you watch a sports programme on TV last night?*

1   visit a friend/yesterday   _____?

2   play football/last week   _____?

3   talk/a minute ago   _____?

4   dance/last weekend   _____?

5   walk/a week ago   _____?

6   phone/two days ago   _____?

7   listen/yesterday   _____?

Use Your Grammar

◼ The past

You can use these verbs to describe past actions:

phone   visit   enjoy   stay   work   watch   listen   talk

Think!

What did you do an hour ago?   Where were you last night?
What did you do yesterday?   Who were you with?
What did you do last week?

Remember to use some time phrases to say **exactly** when things happened in the past – **last** week, **yesterday**, three hours **ago**.

> I **was** in France **last** month. I **visited** a great museum.
> I **was** in Germany last week. I **visited** my aunt. We **watched** some great films and we **discovered** lots of wonderful shops. On the last day we **played** tennis and then I went to a party and **stayed** until midnight. It **was** great!

◻ Adjectives

One way of making what we write more interesting is to make good use of **adjectives**.

- great
- special
- beautiful
- bad
- horrible

When we use different **adjectives** and **comparatives**, our work becomes even more interesting.

- fantastic
- terrible
- worse than
- better than
- more wonderful than
- sadder than

1 **Sarah was on holiday in Australia in April last year. Read the postcard to her friend.**

I am fourteen now – it was my birthday last week! We are on holiday in Brisbane. We are staying in a big hotel. I am with my mum and dad. The weather is fantastic, of course. There are lots of people on the beach every day. We play volleyball on the beach in the morning and in the evening we watch a show at the hotel. I love my holiday! See you soon,
Love
Sarah

2 Now answer the questions.

1 How old was Sarah last summer? _____

2 Where was she? _____

3 Who was she with? _____

4 Where did they stay? _____

5 Was the weather good? _____

6 Were there lots of people on the beach? _____

7 What did they do in the morning? _____

8 What did they do in the evening? _____

9 Did Sarah like her holiday? _____

3 Read about Catherine's holiday and complete the sentences with the verbs in brackets in the simple past.

Last summer I was on holiday in Spain. We've got a house in Barcelona and I go there every year but last

summer was really special. My friends John and Marina (0) *stayed* (stay) with us and we (1) _____

(visit) lots of beautiful places. My favourite one was the beach at Pals but John really (2) _____ (like)

the cake shop in Gerona! Marina (3) _____ (enjoy) swimming in the sea but it was very cold!

We (4) _____ (play) volleyball on the beach every day with some children from the village. Every

evening after dinner, we (5) _____ (dance) in the disco. I'm not very good at dancing but Marina is

better than me. It was great!

It was a fantastic holiday and I was really sad when it (6) _____ (finish).

4 Now write about a holiday or weekend you enjoyed last year.

_____

_____

_____

_____

_____

_____

_____

_____

_____

_____

_____

_____

Test Yourself

1 **Complete the sentences with the correct form of the verb in brackets.**

0   I play football on Sundays, but yesterday I *played* volleyball.   (play)

1   I like cartoons on television, but last night I _____ a film.   (watch)

2   She _____ Jim last year and she still _____ him now.   (love)

3   Claudia can _____ very high. Last week she _____ 1.35 metres.   (jump)

4   We often _____ our cousins. We _____ them a week ago.   (visit)

5   A year ago Jane _____ in Italy. Now, she _____ in Australia.   (live)

6   My mum can _____ lovely meals, but last night she _____ a terrible one.   (cook)

7   Bill _____ his father's car every week. He _____ it two days ago.   (wash)

2 **Put apostrophes in the correct places. Then write the words with apostrophes in full.**

0   Marina **didn't** play tennis yesterday.   *did not*

1   Antonio wasnt at school today.   _____

2   John and Paul werent at home when I phoned.   _____

3   Did you like that film? No, I didnt.   _____

4   Jim didnt want to go home.   _____

5   The weather wasnt very nice last week.   _____

3 **Underline the correct word(s).**

0   Carla **not wanted/<u>didn't want</u>** to dance.

1   Did they **play/played** volleyball when they were small?

2   Some people **not escaped/didn't escape** from the volcano in Pompeii.

3   The race **started/start** at two o'clock.

4   Anna looked in the garden, but her dog **wasn't/weren't** there.

5   The dog **was/did** in the garden.

6   **Did/was** Helen enjoy the party?

7   Did they like their holiday? No, they **weren't/didn't**.

4 Tick the correct sentences.

0   Did she like her present?   ✓

1   Yes, she liked.   ☐

2   Did you buy a new tracksuit?   ☐

3   Yes, I did buy.   ☐

4   What did happened yesterday?   ☐

5   We visited the zoo yesterday.   ☐

6   Did they enjoyed the football match?   ☐

7   Yes, they did.   ☐

8   Was you at school last week?   ☐

9   Yes, I was.   ☐

10   Were your friends at school, too?   ☐

11   Yes, they did.   ☐

5 Underline the correct answer.

0   Yesterday I _____ basketball.
    a. play   b. did played   c. played

1   Sue and Harry are watching TV.
    They _____ TV last night, too.
    a. watch   b. watched   c. didn't watch

2   We were at the cinema _____.
    a. last night   b. night ago   c. last day

3   I _____ my cousin a week ago.
    a. visited   b. visit   c. visits

4   It _____ Dan's birthday last week.
    a. did   b. was   c. were

5   My mum talked to my teacher a _____.
    a. last week   b. week ago   c. week past

8 GHOSTS

Look at **page 5** of this book to find all the **irregular** verbs

LESSON 1 — *I saw them on the Ghost Train*

Past simple: irregular verbs: affirmative

Irregular verbs do not have the ending **–ed** in the **past simple** – so you have to learn them one by one.

Let's look at the verb **go** in the **past simple**:

Affirmative
I went
you went
he went
she went
it went
we went
you went
they went

Look at **page 5** of this book to find all the **irregular** verbs that we use in **Shine Grammar 1**.

---

1 **Match.**

0	1	2	3	4	5	6	7	8
can	see	say	go	write	get	find	do	have
d	☐	☐	☐	☐	☐	☐	☐	☐

a	b	c	d	e	f	g	h	i
said	had	found	~~could~~	saw	did	went	wrote	got

2 **Complete the sentences with the verbs in brackets in the simple past.**

0 This book is very good. I *read* (read) it last night.

1 George _____ a bike to school this morning. (ride)

2 Claudia _____ a beautiful dress to the dance last night. (wear)

3 Jim looked everywhere for his pen. He _____ it in his bag. (find)

4 My grandfather _____ to visit us yesterday. (come)

5 My dad _____ to my teacher. (speak)

6 When I _____ to Budapest, I _____ a new jacket. (go) (get)

7 Rosa _____ the race yesterday. (win)

3 **Read about Lara's bad day.**

Complete the sentences with the correct form of these verbs.

can drink feel get get ~~have~~ have run say see stand

Yesterday I (0) *had* a really bad morning. I (1) _____ up late. I only (2) _____ an apple for

breakfast and I (3) _____ some cold tea. Then I looked out of the window. I (4) _____ see

my bus! I (5) _____ to the bus stop and I (6) _____ on the bus, but it was full so I

(7) _____ all the way to school. I (8) _____ terrible. Then my friend (9) _____ me.

She (10) _____ 'Don't worry. Our teacher is late today, too!'

4 **Read the text again and underline the mistake in each sentence. Then correct it.**

0	Yesterday Lara had a good day.	*Yesterday Lara had a bad day.*
1	She went to bed late.	_____
2	She had a banana.	_____
3	She drank some hot coffee.	_____
4	She looked out of the door.	_____
5	She could see the train.	_____
6	She walked to the bus stop.	_____
7	She sat down all the way to school.	_____
8	She felt good.	_____
9	Her teacher was early.	_____

5 **Underline the correct answer.**

0   Claudia _____ two glasses of cola.
    a <u>drank</u>   **b** drink   **c** drinked

1   Bill _____ all the way home.
    a run   **b** runned   **c** ran

2   I _____ to my friend's house for dinner.
    a go   **b** went   **c** wented

3   We _____ TV at Maria's house.
    a watch   **b** watched   **c** wore

4   My penfriend _____ a long letter to me.
    a wrote   **b** writed   **c** write

5   Sarah _____ football with her friends.
    a play   **b** playing   **c** played

6   Catherine _____ some magazines to her friend in hospital.
    a took   **b** take   **c** taked

7   Jim _____ a new tracksuit.
    a want   **b** went   **c** wanted

Where did you go?

Past simple: regular and irregular verbs: negative and questions

We make the **negative** for **regular** and **irregular** verbs in the **past simple** by using the auxilary verb **didn't** (**did not**) + the **main verb**. We don't change the main verb at all.

Negative (Regular)
I didn't like the sea.
You didn't like the sea.
He didn't like the sea.
She didn't like the sea.
It didn't like the sea.
We didn't like the sea.
You didn't like the sea.
They didn't like the sea.

Negative (Irregular)
I didn't go to the party.
You didn't go to the party.
He didn't go to the party.
She didn't go to the party.
It didn't go to the party.
We didn't go to the party.
You didn't go to the party.
They didn't go to the party.

Good news - it's the same for **questions**!
We use the word **did** to help us make **questions**.

Questions (Regular)
Did I like the beach?
Did you like the beach?
Did he like the beach?
Did it like the beach?
Did we like the beach?
Did you like the beach?
Did they like the beach?

Questions (Irregular)
Did I go to the party?
Did you go to the party?
Did he go to the party?
Did it go to the party?
Did we go to the party?
Did you go to the party?
Did they go to the party?

Now have a look at how we use these **question words** – **what**, **why**, **who**, **where**, **when**, **which** – when we make **past simple** questions.

What did you learn yesterday?
Who did he meet last night?
When did you see that film?

Why didn't she do her homework?
Where did they go last Friday?
Which film did you enjoy more?

---

1 Complete the sentences.

0 Did you go to the cinema last night?

Yes, I *went* to the cinema.

1 Did you meet a friend at the cinema?

Yes, I _____ my friend Andrea.

2 Did you see *Tarzan*?

No, we _____ *Tarzan*.

We _____ a different film.

3 What did you see?

We _____ *Batman III.*

4 Did you like it?

Yes, I did. But Andrea _____ it.

5 Did you have a drink?

No, we _____ any drinks.

6 Did you read about the film in the newspaper?

Yes, I _____ about it in

the newspaper.

7 Did you write about it at school?

No, I _____ about it at school.

2 Write questions. Then write short answers and full answers.

0   he/watch/the film today?
    Did he watch the film today? No, he didn't. He watched the film yesterday.

1   she/eat/a hamburger today?

_____

2   they/take/all their bags today?

_____

3   your mum/speak/to your teacher today?

_____

4   you/write/a letter to your penfriend today?

_____

5   he/finish/his homework today?

_____

3 Write questions for these answers.

0   Where *did you go?*   I went to the cinema.

1   Which cinema _____ ? We went to the ABC cinema.

2   Who _____ ? I went with Andrea and Bill.

3   What time _____ ? The film started at half past seven.

4   What did _____ ? We went to a friend's house for some pizza.

5   When did _____ ? I came home after the pizza. It was late.

4 Yesterday Arnie was in the space station. Make these sentences affirmative.

0   He didn't go into a spaceship.   *He went into a spaceship.*

1   He didn't see a big computer.   _____

2   He didn't have a ride in space.   _____

3   He couldn't float.   _____

4   He didn't find a camera.   _____

5   He didn't take a photo of the stars.   _____

6   He didn't have a shower.   _____

7   He didn't go to Hula-Hula to see his mum and dad. _____

8   He didn't say good-bye to his mum and dad.   _____

9   He didn't come back to Earth.   _____

LESSON 3 — *Why did you scream?*

❶ Questions: *Why ...? Because ...*

We use the question word **Why** when we want to know the reason for something.
> **Why** are you running?

When we use **why** in **past simple questions**, we want to know the reason for something that happened in the past.
> **Why** did you phone Rose yesterday?

We can make **negative** questions too – by using **didn't**.
> **Why didn't** you answer my question?

The **answer** to **Why** questions begins with the word **Because**.
> **Why** didn't you answer my question?
> **Because** I didn't understand it.

❷ *Too + adjective/adverb*

The word **too** doesn't just mean **very**. It means more than is good.
> My coffee is **too** hot. (I can't drink it)
> He drove **too** fast. (It was dangerous)

❸ *Very + adjective/adverb*

We use **very** for emphasis.
> Nick is **very** tall.

Very isn't like the word **too**. There is no problem with Nick being tall – we just want to say that he is taller than a lot of people his age.

---

1 Match.

0	Why did you scream?	**d** — a Because it's exciting.
1	Why don't you buy this tracksuit?	☐ — b Because it was interesting.
2	Why aren't you watching the programme?	☐ — c Because he sings beautifully.
3	Why did you read this book?	☐ — ~~d Because I saw a ghost.~~
4	Why didn't you get up early?	☐ — e Because she wasn't very fast.
5	Why are you going to the fair?	☐ — f Because it's too expensive.
6	Why didn't she win the race?	☐ — g Because I went to bed late.
7	Why is he successful?	☐ — h Because it's too boring.

2 Mario is not a good student and he never does his homework. Answer the questions with verbs in the past.

Teacher: Why didn't you give me your homework?

0 Because *my baby sister took it.*   baby sister/take

1 Because _____   dog/eat

2 Because _____   feel sick/yesterday

3 Because _____   mum/wash

4 Because _____   dad/take/to work

5 Because _____   be boring

6 Because _____   can (not)/understand

3 Put the words in the right order.

0 bus he Why did off get the?   *Why did he get off the bus?*

1 didn't Why you for wait me? _____

2 you late Because were too. _____

3 going car too is fast That. _____

4 want I don't run to – it's hot too! _____

5 played She the beautifully guitar _____

6 Why laughing you are? _____

7 you Because funny look very! _____

4 Complete the sentences with *very* or *too*.

0 Well I think he's *very* silly.

1 You can't watch this film – you're _____ young.

2 I don't want to go to the disco – I'm _____ tired.

3 I couldn't stop my bike because I was going _____ fast.

4 Look at that tiger. It looks _____ strong.

5 I can't carry your bag – it's _____ heavy.

6 I love this programme because it's _____ funny.

7 Tom is taller than Martin. He's _____ tall.

Use Your Grammar

🗊 Stories

We often use the **past simple tense** when we want to tell stories.

Do you remember how we make the **past simple** for both **regular** and **irregular** verbs?
Do you remember how we make **past simple** questions and negative sentences?
If you don't – look back through the unit – then try to use the **past simple** when you write stories.

🗊 Because

When we want to explain the reason for something we can use **because.**

I went to London **because** I wanted to see Buckingham Palace.

1 Complete the story with the correct form of the verb in brackets.

It was 1st April and Tom's birthday. He was really excited because his mum and dad (0) *gave* (give) him a new bike. He (1) _____ (finish) his breakfast quickly and

(2) _____ (ride) the bike to school. After school he (3) _____ (play) football with his friends in the park and when he (4) _____ (come) home it was late and very dark.

Suddenly he (5) _____ (see) a strange white light and he (6) _____ (follow) it. It was a girl on a pink horse. She (7) _____ (have) long blue hair and a green face. The girl (8) _____ (take) him to a big red house on top of a mountain. He (9) _____ (go) inside and (10) _____ (see) lots of people with green faces and blue hair. 'This is really funny', he said. 'Am I asleep?' He (11) _____ (look) around and (12) _____ (see) his friends from school and his mum and dad. 'Surprise!', they all (13) _____ (shout). 'Happy Birthday, Tom! April Fool!'

2 **Now write your own story.**

3 **Answer the questions (you can use your imagination).**

1   Where were you yesterday?

_____

2   Who was with you?

_____

3   What was the weather like?

_____

4   What did you eat?

_____

5   What did you do?

_____

6   Why did you do it?

_____

7   How did you feel?

_____

8   What happened at the end of the day?

_____

8 GHOSTS

LESSON 5 *Test Yourself*

1 Underline the correct answer.

0 We **got/get** off the bus in the centre of town last night.
1 We **flew/flied** to New York last week.
2 He **run/ran** all the way home yesterday.
3 She **weared/wore** a beautiful dress yesterday evening.
4 I **felt/feeled** very scared when I saw the ghost.
5 She **write/wrote** a letter to her friend yesterday.
6 I **read/readed** a great book last night.
7 We **see/saw** a fantastic film yesterday.
8 He **go/went** home early last night.
9 She **sitted/sat** down in the big chair.

2 Look at exercise 1 again and write negative sentences.

0 *We didn't get off the bus in the centre of town last night.*

1 _____

2 _____

3 _____

4 _____

5 _____

6 _____

7 _____

8 _____

9 _____

3 Complete the sentences with these words.

| because did didn't too why |

0 *Why* do you like old films?
1 I _____ go to the park yesterday.
2 Please close the window – it's _____ cold in here.
3 I want to be an astronaut _____ I love space.
4 _____ they go to the disco last night?
5 She _____ buy any new shoes yesterday.
6 They went to bed _____ they were very tired.
7 _____ didn't you watch that programme last night?
8 Can I open the window? I'm _____ hot!
9 _____ you like your present?

84

4 Write these sentences in the past.

This summer	Last summer
0 We have eggs for breakfast every day. (bananas)	*We had bananas for breakfast every day.*
1 He speaks to his grandfather every day. (girlfriend)	_____
2 She wears her trainers every day. (pink T-shirt)	_____
3 We hear birds singing every day. (Ricky Martin)	_____
4 That boy tells jokes every day. (lies)	_____
5 They don't swim every day. (dance)	_____
6 He sees his friends every day. (brothers)	_____
7 I eat an apple every day. (bar of chocolate)	_____

5 Now write questions for your sentences about last year.

0 *Did we have bananas for breakfast every day?*

1 _____?

2 _____?

3 _____?

4 _____?

5 _____?

6 _____?

7 _____?

6 Write sentences.

0 I eat/crisps at the cinema   yesterday/chocolate

I usually eat crisps at the cinema but yesterday I ate chocolate.

1 he/go to bed early   last night/midnight

2 she/dance/at parties   last Saturday/at the disco

3 we/have picnic/in the mountains   last Sunday/at the beach

4 they/go/to Las Vegas   last summer/to Florida

5 you/cook/pizza   last night/spaghetti

LESSON 1 — *It never rains*

Adverbs of frequency

always   usually   often   sometimes   never

I **always** brush my teeth in the morning. (every day)
I **usually** drink milk for breakfast. (almost every day)
I **often** help my friend with his homework. (more days than not)
I **sometimes** ride my bike. (on some days, but not most days)
I **never** forget to do my English homework. (on no days)

Where do we put the **adverbs of frequency**?
We put **adverbs of frequency** in front of the main verb in a sentence.
   It **always** snows in winter.
   They don't **often** have parties at their house.

We put **adverbs of frequency** in front of adjectives.
   It's **never** hot in Alaska.
   Tom is **usually** late for class.

1 Tick the correct sentences.

0   My grandfather always gives me a present for my birthday.   ✔

1   She is always a good friend.   ☐

2   They go often to an island in summer.   ☐

3   We take usually a picnic with us.   ☐

4   We are always happy to see our grandparents.   ☐

5   My dad never gets up late.   ☐

6   Our friends sometimes are too busy to play with us.   ☐

2 Complete for you.

1   I _____ have hamburgers for breakfast.

2   I _____ read a book in bed.

3   I _____ help my mother with the shopping.

4   I _____ watch television in the evening.

5   I _____ play basketball.

6   I am _____ nice to my teacher.

7   I _____ see my friends at the weekend.

8   I _____ clean my teeth every day.

9   I _____ study hard and learn my lessons.

10 I am _____ late for school.

3 **Write negative sentences with the words in brackets. Angie the Alien does some very strange things ...**

0   She *doesn't often clean* her teeth.   (often)
    She usually cleans her teeth on Sundays.

1   She _____ spaghetti for breakfast. (always)
    She sometimes eats pizza for breakfast.

2   She _____ football at night.   (usually)
    She usually plays the guitar at night.

3   She _____ at night.   (often)
    She usually sleeps in the day.

4   She _____ trainers.   (usually)
    She usually wears blue shoes.

4 **Put the words in the right order.**

0   usually It is in village that cold   *It is usually cold in that village.*

1   on the bus I see my friends often   _____

2   a dance lesson on Thursday have We always   _____

3   at the weekend sometimes My grandparents visit us _____

4   busy It is in this café always   _____

5   usually There are here lots of people   _____

6   swim I never in winter   _____

7   his dad George helps at the weekend sometimes   _____

8   She in the evening is often at home   _____

LESSON 2 | *And the best dancer is ...*

Superlative adjectives: *–est, most, the best, the worst*

We use the **superlative** form of the adjective when we want to compare more than two things, people or situations.

We make the **superlative** by adding **–est** to adjectives of one or two syllables, and we add **the** before the **superlative**.

     fast – **the** fast**est**

     slow – **the** slow**est**

There are some spelling rules – just like the rules we use for the **comparative** form (when we add **–er**).

     For adjectives that end in **–e**, we only add **–st** to make the **superlative**.

     nice – **the** nice**st**

     For adjectives with one syllable, that end in a vowel and a consonant, we double the last consonant.

     hot – **the** hot**test**

     For adjectives that end in a consonant and **y**, we take away the **y** and add **–iest**.

     funny – **the** funn**iest**

     Don't forget the irregular adjectives:

     good – **the best**

     bad – **the worst**

To make the superlative of adjectives with more than two syllables, we use **the most**.

     beautiful – **the most** beautiful

     exciting – **the most** exciting

---

1 Complete the sentences with the superlative form of the adjectives.

0   Maths is difficult, but science is *the most difficult* lesson.

1   English is easy, but Italian is _____ language.

2   Catherine is pretty, but Christina is _____ girl in the class.

3   Peter is fast, but Jack is _____ runner in the school.

4   Volleyball is exciting, but basketball is _____ sport.

5   McEnroe was successful, but Sampras was _____ tennis player in the world.

6   Michael Owen is a great English football player, but David Beckham is _____

7   *Dijimon* is interesting, but *Pokemon* is _____ programme.

2 Look and write sentences.

expensive

0   A *video player is expensive. A CD player is more expensive than a video player. A computer is the most expensive.*

1   **big**

_____

_____

2   **short**

_____

_____

3   **fast**

_____

_____

3 Complete the sentences with these words.

| best | cleverer | cleverest | friendliest |
| most interesting | ~~nicest~~ | | |

There are lots of nice people at my school but

Emily is the (0) ____nicest____ because she always

listens to our problems.

Alex is (1) _____ than most of my friends –

he is very good at science and maths. But Nick is

the (2) _____ because he always gets top

marks. He is the (3) _____ student in the

school. Marianna knows everybody. Last year she

won a prize for the (4) _____ person in the

school. Peter is the (5) _____ because he

has so many different hobbies.

4 Underline the mistake in each sentence. Then correct it.

0   Marina is the <u>good</u> dancer in the school.
Marina is the best dancer in the school.

1   Nick's party was the more enjoyable.

_____

2   Stella is the friendlier person I know.

_____

3   Marco is best runner in our school.

_____

4   Angela is cleverer from me.

_____

5   Steve was the most happy boy in the class.

_____

LESSON 3 *Are you going to write?*

Future: *going to*

We use **going to** to talk about future plans and to say what we think is going to happen in the future.

We form the **going to** future with the **present continuous** of the verb **go + main verb**.

Affirmative	**Negative**	**Questions**
I am going to eat fish.	I'm not going to eat fish.	Am I going to eat fish?
You are going to eat fish.	You're not going to eat fish.	Are you going to eat fish?
He is going to eat fish.	He's not going to eat fish.	Is he going to eat fish?
She is going to eat fish.	She's not going to eat fish.	Is she going to eat fish?
It is going to eat fish.	It's not going to eat fish.	Is it going to eat fish?
We are going to eat fish.	We're not going to eat fish.	Are we going to eat fish?
You are going to eat fish.	You're not going to eat fish.	Are you going to eat fish?
They are going to eat fish.	They're not going to eat fish.	Are they going to eat fish?

Questions	**Short answers**
Are you going to see Laura tonight?	Yes, I am./No, I'm not.
Is Mary going to have a party?	Yes, she is./No, she isn't.
Are they going to travel to India?	Yes, they are./No, they aren't.

Top Tip!
You don't change the main verb at all when you use **going to** to talk about the future.
Remember to change the word order when you make questions.

---

1 **Complete the sentences with the verbs in brackets and** *going to.*

0 Tom *is going to play* with his friends this evening. (play)

1 Sandra _____ to her penfriend. (write)

2 My mum and dad _____ to the cinema tomorrow. (go)

3 I _____ my new dress to the disco. (wear)

4 We _____ in a big hotel on our holiday. (stay)

5 They _____ the race soon. (start)

2 **Put the words in the right order.**

0 going the zoo to We're go to today.   *We're going to go to the zoo today.*

1 come They're not disco going to to the. _____

2 Are us? they going wait to for _____

3 I'm to a football match watch on Saturday going. _____

4 in Is this she going to run race? _____

5 grandfather?Are see going you to your _____

3 **What is Andy going to do today? What isn't he going to do?**
Look and write sentences.

0   *He's going to read a magazine.*

1   _____

2   _____

3   _____

4   _____

5   _____

4 **Look at exercise 3 again and write questions and short answers.**

0   *Is Andy going to read a magazine?*   *Yes, he is.*

1   _____ ?   _____

2   _____ ?   _____

3   _____ ?   _____

4   _____ ?   _____

5   _____ ?   _____

5 **What are you going to do at the weekend?**
Write sentences.

I'm going to   _____

I'm not going to   _____

I'm going to   _____

I'm not going to   _____

9 AROUND THE WORLD

LESSON 4 *Use Your Grammar*

1 Future: *going to*

At the New Year, people plan for the future. We can use **going to** to talk about our plans.

    I am **going to** learn ten new words every day!

    I am **going to** visit Paris.

Think!

Think about your plans for the summer. Now you can talk or write about them using **going to**.

2 Superlative

Sometimes we use the **basic** adjective.

    Sarah is **beautiful**.

Sometimes we want to compare two things and we use the **comparative**.

    Sarah is **more beautiful than** her sister.

Sometimes we want to compare more than two things and we use the **superlative**.

    Sarah is the **most beautiful** girl in her class.

1 **Complete the sentences with the verbs in brackets in the correct tense.**

I'm really excited because this summer I'm (0) *going to go* (go) to Camp with all my friends.

I (1) _____ (go) to one last year but I (2) _____ (be) only ten years

old then and it was really boring. This year (3) _____ (be) fantastic.

There (4) _____ (be) a big old house where we usually eat but I hope we

(5) _____ (sleep) outside - under the stars in our sleeping bags.

There is a swimming pool and a beautiful beach. I can't swim but I'm (6) _____

(learn) if the water is not too cold. All my friends can swim but last year I (7) _____

(be) too scared.

There is a disco and we (8) _____ (dance) there every night. We are going to be the

best dancers!

I (9) _____ (miss) my mum and dad and my cat, too, but I (10)

_____ (meet) lots of new friends. I know I (11) _____ (have) a

really good time.

2 Match.

1	My mum is the most	a	football player in his school.
2	Anne is the fastest	b	is volleyball.
3	English is the most	c	beautiful woman I know.
4	Michael is the worst	d	is maths.
5	The best sport	e	runner in her class.
6	My worst subject at school	f	enjoyable lesson at school!

3 Make sentences.

0   I / visit / my grandmother / this weekend.
    I am going to visit my grandmother this weekend.

1   they / play / football / this evening.

_____

2   you / watch / TV / tomorrow?

_____

3   mum and dad / go / to a concert / on Saturday.

_____

4   we / have / spaghetti / tonight?

_____

5   she / have / a party / next month.

_____

6   he / wait / for us / near the cinema?

_____

4 Write about what you are going to do this weekend.

_____

_____

_____

_____

_____

_____

_____

_____

_____

1 Write questions about Maria's friends. Use *who* or *which* and the correct form of the word in brackets.

0	*Who is the fastest* swimmer?	(fast)
1	_____ basketball player?	(good)
2	_____ place? The café or the restaurant?	(nice)
3	_____ lives _____ to the sports centre?	(near)
4	_____? Computer games or the cinema?	(interesting)
5	_____ sport?	(bad)

2 Write short answers about yourself.

1 Can you play the guitar? _____

2 Do you like swimming? _____

3 Are you a fast runner? _____

4 Were you in bed at eleven o'clock this morning? _____

5 Have you got a nice teacher? _____

6 Are you writing the answers now? _____

7 Did you watch a film yesterday? _____

8 Are you going to see an alien tomorrow? _____

9 Did you do all your homework last night? _____

10 Are you better at English than your friend? _____

3 Complete with the correct form of the verb in brackets.

0   I am *going to win* the race tomorrow!   (win)

1   He _____ his homework now.   (do)

2   They usually _____ swimming every day.   (go)

3   She's very good at _____ .   (dance)

4   Did you _____ a taxi home yesterday?   (take)

5   I never _____ tennis. It's too boring.   (play)

6   We don't like _____ old films.   (watch)

7   I _____ my friends at the fair yesterday evening. (see)

8   Are you _____ to this CD?   (listen)

9   He sometimes _____ long stories.   (read)

10 We _____ to the cinema last night.   (go)

4 Complete the sentences with these words.

| How   What   When   Where   Which   Who   Why |

0   *What* are you going to do tomorrow?

1   _____ didn't you do your homework?

2   _____ computer game do you like best?

3   _____ are you going to come to my house?

4   _____ is your best friend?

5   _____ many videos has he got?

6   _____ time does our maths lesson start?

7   _____ do you like basketball?

8   _____ do you live?

9   _____ old is your brother?

10 _____ is going to come to your party?

Macmillan Education
Between Towns Road, Oxford OX4 3PP
A division of Macmillan Publishers Limited
Companies and representatives throughout the world

ISBN 0 333 99993 2

First published 2002

Designed by Sofia Flokou

Illustrated by: Kath Abbott (Specsart); Alan Batson (Specsart); Mike
Bell (Specsart); Roger Blackwell (Specsart); Mark Duffin; Bob Harvey
(Pennant); Gillian Hunt; Tim Kahan; Helen Kidd (Posters); Angela
Lumley (Specsart); Mark MacLaughlin; Des Nicholas; Julia Pearson;
Glynn Rees (Specsart); Paul Shorrock; Dan Simpson (Specsart); Gary
Slater; Simon Turner; Roger Wade Walker.

Cover design by Xen Media Ltd

The authors would like to thank: Sue Jones, Lidia Kacelnik, Julie
Stone and all at Macmillan Education with special thanks to Kathy
Mestheneou for all her hard work.

Thank you, too, to Alberto, Cristina and Matteo for their patience
and to Hayley, Angela and Colleen for all the extra child-minding!

The authors and publishers would like to thank the following for
permission to use the photographic images: Collections p41, Corbis
Royalty free pp72, 87; Digital Stock pp42, 43; Getty Images p52, 62(b),
64, 65; Image Bank p12; Oxford Scientific Films pp37, 75.

Commissioned photography by: Peter Lake pp 7, 8, 9, 15, 19, 22, 24,
27(t, m), 28, 32, 33, 35, 40, 45, 62(t), 67, 69, 70, 71, 77, 89(ml, mm, mr).

Additional Photography by: Haddon Davis pp 6, 20, 21, 31, 36, 44,
48, 57, 89(tl, tm, tr), 91: Debbie Hughes p27(b).

Printed and bound in Spain by Edelvives S. A.
2005   2004   2003   2002
10 9 8 7 6 5 4 3 2 1